FROM THE COCHABAMBA MANIFESTO

Cochabambinos, Cochabambinas—you cannot beg for civil rights. Rights are won in struggle. No one else is going to fight for what is ours. Either we fight together for justice or we let bad rulers humiliate us. (January 10, 2000)

THE COCHABAMBA DECLARATION

We, citizens of Bolivia, Canada, United States, India, Brazil—farmers, workers, indigenous people, students, professionals, environmentalists, educators, nongovernmental organizations, retired people, gather together today in solidarity to combine forces in the defense of the vital right to water.

Here, in this city which has been an inspiration to the world for its retaking of that right through civil action, courage, and sacrifice—standing as heroes and heroines against corporate, institutional and governmental abuse, and trade agreements which destroy that right, in use of our freedom and dignity, we declare the following:

For the right to life, for the respect of nature and the uses and traditions of our ancestors and our peoples, for all time the following shall be declared as inviolable rights with regard to the uses of water given us by the earth:

1. Water belongs to the earth and all species and is sacred to life, therefore, the world's water must be conserved, reclaimed, and protected for all future generations and its natural patterns respected.

2. Water is a fundamental human right and a public trust to be guarded by all levels of government, therefore, it should not be commodified, privatized, or traded for commercial purposes. These rights must be enshrined at all levels of government. In particular, an international treaty must ensure these principles are incontrovertible.

3. Water is best protected by local communities and citizens who must be respected as equal partners with governments in the protection and regulation of water. Peoples of the earth are the only vehicle to promote earth democracy and save water. (December 8, 2000)

¡COCHABAMBA!

¡COCHABAMBA!

WATER WAR IN BOLIVIA

OSCAR OLIVERA

IN COLLABORATION WITH
TOM LEWIS

SOUTH END PRESS
CAMBRIDGE, MASSACHUSETTS

Cover design by Elizabeth Elsas
Text design by Alexander Dwinell, South End Press collective
Cover photos by Tom Kruse

Printed in Canada by union labor on acid-free, recycled paper!

Library of Congress Cataloging-in-Publication Data

Olivera, Oscar.
Cochabamba! : water war in Bolivia / Oscar Olivera, in collaboration with Tom Lewis.
  p. cm.
Includes index.
ISBN 0-89608-702-6 (pbk.: alk. paper)
ISBN 0-89608-703-4 (hardcover: alk. paper)
1. Water-supply—Bolivia—Cochabamba. 2. Government, Resistance to—Bolivia—Cochabamba—Case studies. 3. Privatization—Bolivia—Cochabamba. 4. Natural resources—Bolivia—Management—Citizen participation—Case studies. I. Lewis, Tom, 1950– II. Title.

HD4465.B5O45 2004
333.91'22'098423—dc22

2004019165

South End Press, 7 Brookline Street, #1, Cambridge, MA 02139-4146
www.southendpress.org

09 08 07 06 05 04   1 2 3 4 5 6 7

TABLE OF CONTENTS

This book is dedicated to

Camila, Natali,
Juan José, Devyn, Diego, Grant,
Libertad, and Solidaridad

WATER DEMOCRACY

Vandana Shiva

It was in April 2000—just days after the people of Bolivia's victory in the Water War and just months after popular pressure caused the collapse of the WTO ministerial in Seattle—that I first met Oscar Olivera. The International Forum on Globalization was holding a teach-in at a Washington DC church as part of the A16 protests of the World Bank meetings. Oscar was a last minute addition to the schedule. We did not know, because of the explosive situation in Bolivia, whether he would be able to come to the US and join us. Maude Barlow was speaking and only Ralph Nader and I had yet to speak. Then, direct from the airport, in the rear of the packed church was Oscar. Maude Barlow announced "Our hero from Bolivia has arrived" and the crowd gave Oscar a three minute standing ovation as he made his way to the front.

We met again in 2003 when Oscar came to India to offer solidarity to our struggles for water democracy. I remember him sitting with us in Haridwar, on the bathing ghats on the banks of the Ganges. We strategized around how to strengthen the movement against the privatisation of Ganga water by the world's biggest water giant, Suez. The water for the Suez plant will come from Tehri, where a dam has displaced 100,000 people and buried a civilization. Not only that, the day after the dam flooded the town of Tehri, one of the tunnels of the dam collapsed and killed nearly 60 workers. In Bolivia, as in India and other places around the globe, water issues have clearly become the most urgent life and death issues.

VANDANA SHIVA

Oscar joined us at the National Convention of Water Movements (*Jal Swaraj Abhiyan*) in Delhi. When he showed a film about the struggles in Cochabamba, people cried. The Hindi-speaking activists of India did not feel a barrier in relating to the Spanish-speaking activists and movements of Bolivia. We saw that we were all a part of the same struggle.

I am happy that Oscar Olivera's *¡Cochabamba!* brings the amazing Bolivian experience redefining and reinventing democracy through water and people to a larger community world wide. Oscar, his colleagues and friends in the *Coordinadora de Defensa del Agua y de la Vida* (Coalition in Defense of Water and Life), and the Bolivian people have something very special to teach us about democracy and freedom. From their struggles and victories we are reminded that democracy is not just about elections once every four or five years, but about decisions related to our everyday lives—the food we eat, the water we drink, the livelihoods and jobs we have. As Oscar writes:

> In simple terms, democracy for us answered—and still answers—the question who decides what? A tiny minority of politicians and businesspeople, or we ourselves, the ordinary working people? In the case of Cochabamba's water, we wanted to make our own decisions. That was what democracy would mean in practice, and that was what the *Coordinadora* set out to accomplish.

We also learn through the experience of the people of Cochabamba that real democracy, living democracy, cannot be delegated—to professional politicians, or any one sector of society. It can only be achieved through rainbow coalitions based on trust, not domination and control. As Oscar writes:

> The formation of the *Coordinadora* responded to a political vacuum, uniting peasants, environmental groups, teachers, and blue- and white-collar workers in the manufacturing sector. The *Coordinadora* emerged from the ordinary inhabitants of both town and country who, from an elemental sense of the need to defend such basic rights as access to water, called upon the whole population to join in the struggle. This call was based on understanding the importance of joint actions and believing that no individual sector alone could marshal sufficient strength to block the privatization of water. There could be no individual salvation. Social well-being would be achieved for everyone, or for no one at all.

Oscar Olivera and Álvaro García Linera, a member of the Bolivian intellectual collective *Comuna*, show how capital, through the neo-liberal commodification and privatization of every dimension of life, has simultaneously dissolved the conditions necessary for movements based upon the "union-form," and created, as seen in the new movements for the defense of life, the "multitude-form." Loose, flexible associations of society—in all its diversity—characterize this new type of movement.

The story of Bolivia's Water War and water democracy is not just an inspiration for us all. It also provides political education for every community struggling to reclaim their commons and public spaces in this age of corporate globalization.

If globalization is the ultimate enclosure of the commons—our water, our biodiversity, our food, our culture, our health, our education—then reclaiming the commons is the political, economic, and ecological agenda for our times. *¡Cochabamba!* shows us that a world beyond corporate globalization is not just possible, it is happening. As the Bolivian people remind us, there is one power stronger than the power of money—and that is the power of people.

ABOUT THIS BOOK

¡Cochabamba! presents and analyzes the first great victory against corporate globalization in Latin America. In February and April 2000, hundreds of thousands of ordinary working people in the Andean city of Cochabamba, Bolivia, battled police in the streets in a successful fight to reverse the privatization of the city's water supply.

Part One of this book, "The Water War," tells the story of Cochabamba's struggle in the words of Oscar Olivera. The most prominent leader of the Water War, Oscar brings the ideas and emotions of a first-hand participant to the analysis of events that have inspired activists in social movements around the world. After explaining the process of organizing opposition to the Bolivian government's sale of Cochabamba's water service to a local subsidiary of the US-based Bechtel Corporation, Oscar details the dramatic struggle that eventually defeated the neoliberal privatizers.

Part Two, "Perspectives on the Water War and the *Coordinadora*," provides analysis of Cochabamba's *Coordinadora*, or the Coalition in Defense of Water and Life, and the practical results of victory in the Water War. Mexican activist and intellectual Raquel Gutiérrez Aguilar analyzes the formation and functioning of the *Coordinadora*. Raquel's chapter is followed by an essay by Álvaro García Linera on "the multitude." Álvaro, like Raquel, belongs to the Bolivian intellectual collective *Comuna*, which has significantly influenced the development of Oscar's political ideas. Other principal members of *Comuna* are Luis Tapia and Raúl Prada.

Álvaro here offers a theoretical interpretation of the Cochabamba experience.

Following is an interview with Luis Sánchez-Gómez, who is a member of the executive board of SEMAPA, the restored municipal water company. A report by an international advisory and solidarity committee concludes this section with a study of the water company's progress and needs since the Water War.

In Part Three, "Our Reality and Our Dreams," Oscar discusses the central social and political questions that emerged before, during, and after the Water War. In these chapters, Oscar writes both as a political thinker and as a labor leader. He offers seminal reflections on such issues as the composition of the new working class in Bolivia, old and new models for organizing dissent, the kind of national politics required for genuine democratic self-government, the limitations of the contemporary Bolivian state, the process by which Cochabamba's citizens overcame their fear of repression and gained the confidence to fight, and the necessity of a continent-wide process of social rebellion.

In Part Four, "The Gas War," Oscar examines the contemporary resonance of the Water War in what has come to be known as the Gas War. Indeed, from the Water War to the Gas War, the Bolivian struggle during the first five years of the new millennium has focused on winning popular, democratic control over the country's natural resources. Part Four also includes my essay which chronicles and updates the Bolivian social movement from the Water War to the Gas War.

Texts authored by Oscar for *¡Cochabamba!* derive from taped interviews, speeches, and published articles, which have been revised for the present volume. Luis A. Gómez López, a well-known Mexican journalist living in Bolivia, and I are responsible for Oscar's taped interviews. Both Oscar and I are grateful to Luis for his willingness to share his tapes, on which is based the bulk of Oscar's narration of the Water War. Oscar himself, of course, is responsible for making available his previously published texts as well as the drafts and outlines of his many speeches.

My role as collaborator has included both ghostwriting and translation. I am also responsible for the selection and initial editing of the materials in our volume. The selections and final versions of the materials published here have been reviewed by

Oscar, his sister Marcela Olivera, and Luis Gómez. Obviously, I assume sole responsibility for any errors in chapter composition or translation.

Oscar and I would like to thank Raquel and Álvaro for agreeing to allow Oscar and me to reprint, and me to translate, their articles in *¡Cochabamba!* These valuable texts appear here in English for the first time. We also owe special debts of gratitude to Tom Kruse whose documentary photographs of the Water War appear on the cover of the book and to Tania Quiroz who researched the state of the Bolivian economy. Special thanks are also owed to Alexander Dwinell, Tina Beyene, and the other editors at South End Press, whose patience, exhortation, and belief in the importance of this project endured throughout its rocky road to publication.

I would like to express my deepest gratitude to Marcela Olivera. She conscientiously read and suggested changes for each chapter as it was completed. She served throughout the writing process as a faithful conveyor of Oscar's ideas and as an invaluable resource covering the gaps in my political and cultural knowledge of Bolivia. Over the course of the project, Oscar, Marcela, and I have built a relationship of solidarity and friendship that transcends the pages of this book.

Tom Lewis
August 2004

OF PREFACES, SPACES, AND WRITTEN VOICES

From my mother, the factory, the irrigators, and ordinary working people, I learned that we must all be like water—transparent and in movement. This message has flowed along with me ever since I was a child, student, apprentice, young worker, and combatant and warrior of the streets and roads.

I want to thank all of them: my mother, my sisters and brothers (especially Marcela), my wife, my daughters and sons Camila, Natali, Juan José, Diego, Libertad and Solidaridad (these last two are as identical as two little drops of water); my working sisters and brothers in the factories; my brother Omar and the irrigators; my comrades in the barrios, including the *Barrio 1 de Mayo*; Raquel and Álvaro, the Claudias; the thousands of activists who stand in solidarity as water warriors with us—in and out of the country; all of you who shared and gave me the following values: honesty and struggle, organization and unity, mystique and sacrifice—all those sisters and brothers who I met at the town council, community and mass meetings, spaces where we recuperated our voices, our dignity, our capacity to decide.

Thank you to all who took me in during those moments of anxiety and fear, of desperation and frustration; those of you with whom I shared moments of victory, sweat, and struggle. We all share this history that, in the end, is your history … is our history.

In this fragment of history reflecting our struggle for water, I simply serve as a spokesperson. A large journey still remains ahead of us as we struggle to obtain our desires and our dreams.

My name is Oscar Olivera Foronda. I was born in the state of Oruro, in the Bolivian *altiplano*, in a small town called Agua de Castilla. A few years ago it struck me as significant that my town's name translates as Water of Castile and that my zodiac sign is Aquarius, because I am involved with water as a social issue.

One of ten children, I moved to Cochabamba with my family in 1960 when I was five years old. My father was a military officer and my mother ran a small bakery. When I turned sixteen I began to work in the factories. I've been working in the *Manufacturas Cochabamba* (MANACO) shoe factory in Cochabamba for the last twenty-five years.

I do not belong to any political party, although I should acknowledge that my basic political development started in 1971 or 1972 at a technological institute where I studied. There was a significant presence of social justice activists at the institute during that time. They were engineers and sociologists who communicated an extremely important vision of life that gave meaning to our existence. I linked this vision with the values that my own family transmitted to me. Our father once endured a prolonged period of unemployment and our mother worked outside the home. We were ten children, twelve mouths that had to share food. Each one of us had a role and we supported one another. I believe that these roles taught me the value of solidarity.

At the end of the 1970s, during the final years of the dictatorship of General Hugo Banzer, I worked with a left-wing political party until the defeat of the dictatorship in the early 1980s.

What attracted me to this party was that I felt the organization and the leaders took on a great deal of responsibility, had charisma, and were consistent in their actions. I've always admired the party's leader, D. Federico Escobar Zapata, who is the only working-class leader to have a monument dedicated to him in a historic place in Bolivia. I learned a lot from these militants, not only through their work and political practice, but also through the various texts analyzing working-class politics that I read for the national congresses. The historical presence of Che Guevara in Bolivia also exercised a strong influence on me.

Since 1980 I have been active in the labor movement. I have participated as a rank-and-file delegate, as a leader of my local union, and as a national leader in the Central Obrera Departamental—Cochabamba (COD; Cochabamba State Confederation of Workers). I was also the head of the *Federación de Fabriles* (*Fabriles;* Confederation of Factory Workers of Bolivia), which organizes workers in light industry, during 1989 and 1990.

From 1990 to 1995, at the request of my fellow workers, I again served as leader of my local union. In 1995 there was an intense round of layoffs, and I felt I had to return to a regional leadership post. From 1995 to the present, I have served as the main leader of the *Fabriles* in the state of Cochabamba. I have presided over four recent national workers' congresses held in Cochabamba. I also directed a national congress of factory workers, and I've been a member of the COD's honor board during various negotiations.

In the year 2000, I participated in the Water War and acted as a spokesperson for the *Coordinadora de Defensa del Agua y de la Vida* (Coalition in Defense of Water and Life). We claimed the first space in which men, women, children and the elderly were able to demonstrate, to the country and the world, against the neoliberal policies which had subsumed our lives. The neoliberal model, despite its presence in every aspect of peoples daily existence, was not able to win the hearts of people exhausted by state violence, whose human rights have been taken away, and who are furious at seeing their natural resources of their country given to transnational corporations by our own government.

I have participated in mobilizations that have profoundly affected my life. Four times, with the *cocaleros* (coca growers) and other sectors of society, I have marched hundreds of kilometers to La Paz, the nation's capital. I reached La Paz three of those times. I've been lucky enough to travel to other countries like Brazil, Cuba, Canada, the United States, South Africa, and India where I managed to establish connections with sections of the labor movement.

I think these experiences comprise my political background. More than teaching me a party line, I would say they gave me a basic education. They helped me see the world in a different way from most people, who have not had the possibility or privilege of encountering as many other people, sectors of society, and union leaders that I did, or have not been able to participate in study circles. I do not consider myself a Marxist, a Leninist, or a Maoist.

OSCAR OLIVERA

I am a person who wants to give content and meaning to his life. I believe that life has value in the actions we take. We should say what we want and then work toward that goal with consistency and integrity, without walking away.

I have six children. The eldest is twenty-four, and my youngest—twins—are almost three years old. If I could, if all the changes to which I have dedicated my life were to come to fruition, I would choose to be an ordinary worker. I would contribute my labor to society; I would share the problems and solidarity of my workplace; I would participate in worker's assemblies and debate concrete issues of concern in our factory. I would go home at night, help my kids with their homework, listen to the radio and watch television sitting next to my children, and share the weekends with my wife and family. I would travel and take photographs like I used to do. I would choose a more private, more everyday life. I would be an ordinary worker.

My life hasn't been like this. But I continue to fight so that one day all working men and women, myself and my family included, can experience a lifetime of daily fulfillment and joy.

Hasta la victoria siempre,

Oscar Olivera
Bolivia, one day in 2004

¡THE WATER WAR!

PRIVATIZATION

Neoliberalism and privatization of formerly public resources have not benefited the overwhelming majority of Bolivians. Since the start of the New Economic Policy (NEP) in 1985 there are fewer jobs and more unemployment. Working conditions have deteriorated substantially. Services are becoming more and more expensive. Because of lower revenues and higher costs, the state no longer has enough money to maintain public services. For some time now, because of this and pressure from international lending agencies, the government has sought to privatize the public service sector. After DS 21060 set in motion the privatizing of national industry the government has sought to privatize public services.[1]

In 1999 and 2000—after privatizing many industries, most significantly the mines—the transnationals, the World Bank, and the government mafias attempted to take away our water. They sought to turn this vital resource into a business. But water is a social good, a natural inheritance of all living beings—plants, animals, and humans. We all know this. That is why no one can own water. Thanks to the mobilizations of the people of Cochabamba they did not succeed and, as yet, no one owns Bolivian air and water. But if the corporations and politicians get another chance, they will use any means and will spare no effort to privatize them.

WATER PRIVATIZATION

Cochabamba is a city of more than six hundred thousand people. There are upwards of one million inhabitants including the surrounding area. It is the third largest urban environment in the country. For more than fifty years, we who live in Cochabamba have suffered from a shortage of water. Farmers produce a lot of vegetables in our region, so water problems affect not only drinking water—water for household consumption—but also water for agricultural use. Our water shortages have been historically used by politicians and businesspeople to manipulate the population in pursuit of corporate interests and corporate power.

The Misicuni water project, for example, has been "opened" by three different presidents, each saying that, unlike the others, they would bring the project to fruition.[2] Regional political parties have played one water development project against another in their marketing efforts to get votes.

In June 1999, the World Bank issued a report on Bolivia discussing the water situation in Cochabamba. The World Bank, which along with the International Development Bank had made privatization a condition for loans, recommended that there be "no public subsidies" to hold down increases in the price of water service.[3] This was the perspective of wealthy people living in Washington, for whom a $30 increase in their monthly water bill is nothing. But for many Cochabamban families, where the official minimum wage is 330 bolivanos per month (approximately $41), such an increase would be catastrophic. Yet the Bolivian national government followed the World Bank's recommendation and moved to privatize Cochabamba's water system.

A key component of the government's effort to privatize water was the October 1999 promulgation of Law 2029, which governed drinking water and sanitation. Law 2029 eliminated any guarantee of water distribution to rural areas, a practice in place for so long it was—and still is—considered a custom. The people look at water as something quite sacred. Water is a right for us, not something to be sold. The right to water is also tied to traditional beliefs for rural people, as it has been since the time of the Incas. The traditional social practices and ideas behind the use of water go beyond the distribution of water to encompass the idea that water belongs to the community and no one has the right to own the water. But Law 2029 prohibited traditional water practices.

When Law 2029 was passed on October 29, only half of Cochabamba's population was connected to the central water system. Many others obtained water from cooperative water houses which had been built in each barrio to meet community needs. In other areas, where the people did not have the money to build a well, they bought cisterns.

The autonomous water systems were developed in a variety of ways. Often local neighborhood groups contributed what they could in terms of money and labor to construct the system. Sometimes non-governmental organizations (NGOs) and even the World Bank assisted the development. In many communities there would be a committee with a two-year term that managed the system. All the money paid for water went back into the project. Approximately 80 percent would go to pay the electricity bill for operating the pump and 20 percent would be spent on maintenance. A small salary might be paid to the person who did the paperwork.

Yet Law 2029 stated that within the territory covered by a privatization contract such systems are illegal. Only the contracted company could distribute water. The law thus demanded that the autonomous water systems be handed over without reimbursement or compensation for the people who invested their own time and money to build their own systems. The law went so far as to include wells established in people's houses. If I had a well in my house, I would have to pay to use it—or the company could cap it.

The law also prohibited the peasants from constructing collection tanks to gather water from the rain. The rain, too, had been privatized. Law 2029 required people to ask for permission from the superintendent of water to collect rainwater. The superintendent gave private companies a concession for forty years of general water use while only conceding five years to the irrigators and peasants in the outlying communities.

The privatazation law also hurt the local townships. It eliminated their right to determine where water wells could be dug and it eliminated their ability to collect water taxes. Furthermore, in deference to transnational corporations, it "dollarized" water payments. This didn't mean the people had to pay in US dollars, but if the *boliviano* dropped in value against the dollar their water bill would increase to the equivalent price in US dollars.

Even worse than Law 2029 proved to be the forty-year contract with *Aguas del Tunari* (Tunari Waters) to run the Cochabamba water system. The contract was signed on September 3, 1999, but the details of it did not emerge until *Aguas del Tunari,* which waited until Law 2029 took effect, began operation on November 1. There was a clause in the contract stating that the contract itself superseded any other contract, law, or decree. The contract was signed on behalf of the government by the superintendent of energy, who is nominated by Congress for a ten-year term.

The new water company, *Aguas del Tunari,* was sort of a phantom to us. Registered in the Cayman Islands, it was a consortium of enterprises. Its members at the time were International Water, Abengoa of Spain, and four Bolivian companies. International Water, which is part of the vast holdings of US-based Bechtel Corporation, held the majority interest in the consortium. One of the Bolivian companies belonged to Samuel Doria Medina, the owner of Bolivia's Burger King franchise and a prominent politician in one of the governing parties, the *Movimiento Izquierda Revolucionaria* (MIR; Movement of the Revolutionary Left)—which, despite its name, is neither left nor revolutionary. This meant that the government's interests meshed with those of *Aguas del Tunari.*

The government's contract with *Aguas del Tunari* specified that at the end of each year, rates would go up as measured against the consumer price index in the United States. The contract guaranteed the company an average 16 percent rate of return per year on its investment—no matter how management performed or what quality of service was provided.

Once *Aguas del Tunari* began operation it took advantage of its exclusive rights to water distribution under Law 2029 and announced the confiscation of all existing water networks. Curiously, something else began to happen—at least according to the water company. People were suddenly consuming more water. That is what the water bills said. But everyone knew they were using the same amount as always. Many people still only had access to water for about two hours a day. But there were bills that said water usage increased from 5 cubic meters to 20 cubic meters per person in one month. It simply was not possible. Hence, not only did the price per cubic meter go up, but also the supposed use. *Aguas del Tunari* never sufficiently explained the increases.

In some cases people's water bills skyrocketed as much as 300 percent. A pensioner, or a teacher who made $80 a month, might see his or her bill jump from $5 to $25 a month. It was very hard for people because they did not have the money. As a result, many people simply refused to pay.[4]

Beyond an inability to pay, we Cochabambinos vehemently opposed Law 2029 because, as I said, we believe that water is a natural gift and that its distribution should be considered a public service instead of a business. Water distribution should take into account the needs of the population. It should be designed not from the point of view of mercantile logic and the pursuit of profit, but rather from a perspective that clearly subordinates the business aspects—investment criteria, expansion plans, and rates—to the common interest.

We believe that it is crucial to preserve the social character and the accrued rights of the local water committees, the city's neighborhood cooperatives, and the rural communities. The monopolistic character of the distribution of water as enshrined in Law 2029 cannot adequately serve the public's needs. Indexing water rates to the dollar, moreover, has no other purpose than to insure maximum profitability for transnational corporations at the expense of ordinary working people.

We objected specifically to the concession of Cochabamba's water supply to *Aguas del Tunari*. The process did not follow legal norms, and the contract guaranteed benefits only for the owners—not the Cochabambinos. Hastily cobbled together to take advantage of the fact that no other company had bid on the privatization of Cochabamba's water, *Aguas del Tunari* had a laughable capital base. It was clear to anyone who had eyes to see that the company intended to raise the money needed for investment from the Cochabambinos themselves. *Aguas del Tunari* expected the people to pay for the improvement and expansion of what had been their water system. But now the water and its improved distribution systems would be owned by private capitalists who had put up virtually nothing of their own.

Ultimately, the quarrel over Law 2029 had to do with the nature of government decision-making. Would decisions be made by taking into consideration the interests of the population, or simply by conforming to what foreign financial entities prescribed? We were—and still are—tremendously worried by the fact that the Bolivian government evidently prefers to follow the dictates of the World Bank instead of taking into account what the population views as in its best interests.

The most contentious points of Law 2029 were clearly the monopolistic character of the concession contract, the arbitrary level of consumer cost, and the confiscation of wells and alternative systems of use. In each respect, the government followed the wishes of transnational capital and adopted a posture of confrontation toward us. Their criterion for water distribution was a one-sided, business-centered plan designed to maximize profitability. This was not our criterion. We wanted inexpensive water through the Misicuni project, a centralized system of water service, the expansion of service to unconnected areas, and an abundant supply of drinking water.

The core issues raised by the privatization of water in Cochabamba were who would decide the present and future of the population, of our resources, and of the conditions in which we live and work. We wanted to decide these matters by and for ourselves. In the same way as we were willing to fight if our hopes were snatched away, we were willing to work with the government and the concessionary company if our interests and needs were recognized. But we would not allow *Aguas del Tunari* to get rich off our backs. We categorically refused to accept the perverse imposition of a dictatorship of privilege and moneyed interests.

HISTORY OF PRIVATIZATION IN BOLIVIA

The privatization of water in Cochabamba and its sale to *Aguas del Tunari* was not the first instance of privatization in Bolivia. And Law 2029 was not the first law or decree passed to facilitate privatization. In 1985 President Víctor Paz Estenssoro issued a famous edict known as DS 21060. This keystone of the NEP profoundly changed the national economy and set in motion the process of neoliberal structural adjustment. The avowed economic objective was to put a stop to inflation, which it did. But DS 21060 also advanced a political goal: to destroy the unions and to privatize state-owned companies.

Prior to 1985, Bolivia could boast one of the strongest and most united labor movements in Latin America. Bolivian labor was rooted in the extensive apparatus of the Bolivian state, with the state providing at least 60 percent of the country's employment until DS 21060 took effect. Many strong, state-owned industries existed before DS 21060—including mining, petroleum, telecom-munications, railroads, and airlines—as well as many individual state-owned factories.

At one time, four Bolivian mines produced 25 percent of the Bolivian state's total revenues. Hence, the economy was highly dependent upon the mining sector, and the miners union wielded considerable strength and political influence. Later the mines began to operate at a loss. The collapse of tin prices on the world market in 1985, moreover, coincided with the introduction of neoliberalism into Bolivia. This meant that, at a time when their livelihoods were threatened, the state refused to intervene to defend the miners' jobs and living standards.[5]

In September 1986, the miners' union organized their famous March for Life, which began in the high plateau and covered 200 kilometers on the way toward its goal, La Paz. The march involved thousands of miners, their families, and supporters from other sectors of society. It was a grand protest against the destruction of a protective public sector that had been willing to recognize a strong union.

But the military intervened to halt the march. Without a single shot being fired, the people demobilized. In reality, this was a kind of abdication. The miners gave in to the state, and that is when a new era began in Bolivia. Once the unionized miners were gone, the government moved to privatize the mines and Bolivia's economic and political elite launched an aggressive drive to smash the entire union movement. A new wave of political repression accompanied the harsh economic changes. Today, thanks to this assault, which coincided with a worldwide mining crash, not a single unionized worker remains in the mines.

Not only did the government privatize public industries, it also greatly undervalued them. For example, the government sold a concession for the Huanuni mine and the Vinto metallurgic com-plex to an English company called Allied Deals, PLC for only $14 million while the complex alone, without the mineral rights, was worth $15 million. So the government practically gave the mine away for free.[6] The government has fashioned this kind of deal with everything it owned.

It usually turns out that there is someone in the government—some politician or relative—who happens to be a partner in the company that takes over the privatized enterprise. The father-in-law of former president Jorge Quiroga is a partner in the company that administers the airports. The ex-ambassador to the European Community, Álvaro Moscoso, is one of the top managers in the company that manages the privatized pension fund.

Bolivia has reached a situation where the state has no more businesses to sell. Even the petroleum company, which contributed more than $400 million annually in tax revenues, provides only about $80 million in taxes after the privatization. Furthermore, no one knows where the money from the mines went after the state sold them.

The neoliberal economic model was imposed in Bolivia as part of the national elite's accommodation to reactionary forces at the global level. Working closely with infamous "shock therapist" Jeffrey Sachs, the government of Víctor Paz Estenssoro designed and issued DS 21060, also known as the NEP, in 1985. Gonzalo Sánchez de Lozada served as Paz Estenssoro's chief economic adviser, and it was later under Sánchez de Lozada's first presidency (1993-1997) that the bulk of Bolivia's state-owned industries were privatized. The stated aim of the NEP was to control hyperinflation, in which it succeeded. But it did so by dramatically lowering the living standards of the majority of Bolivians.

Subsequently known as "corporate globalization," this reactionary regroupment catapulted the largest transnational firms, as well as the main international financial institutions, into positions of world dominance. One and only one goal defined the purpose of neoliberalism in Bolivia: to intensify the exploitation of our natural resources in order to increase corporate profits.

As a result of corporate globalization, we Bolivians—like people from all of the world's poorer countries—have been stripped of our material inheritance and natural resources. We have been robbed of the products that Bolivian men and women have collectively built and conserved. The transnationals have stolen our airplanes, our railways, our roads, our communications, our hydrocarbons, our factories, and our land.

By the end of the 1990s, it was obvious that all ordinary working Bolivians had to show for the years of neoliberalism was greater poverty among the people. All of us had become aware that economic conditions for the general population had deteriorated substantially. Not only were pay increases frozen, but salaries were continuously lowered and had lost their former purchasing power. The discretional, ongoing price increases in basic services gradually converted services such as electricity, education, and health care into luxuries that only a few could enjoy. Indexing the cost of services to the dollar; the rise in the price of hydrocarbons, especially gas; that out of the thousands of factory workers in Cochabamba only a small percent had received even the stingiest salary increase—all of this revealed the panorama of anguish and anxiety that filled the lives of working class families.

THE TYRANNY OF THE EXTERNAL DEBT

Crushing debt service has gone hand in hand with the imposition of neoliberalism throughout Latin America. The vicious cycle of debt Bolivia has been forced into by global capitalism places a chokehold on any chance ordinary working Bolivians may have. From any point of view, this external debt is unpayable and immoral. It has not benefited our peoples in any way. It was contracted undemocratically—in our name, but without our consent. And even if we were able to elect a government that promised to end neoliberalism, such a government would possess only scarce resources for improving living standards as long as it continued to service the debt.

If the objective of the international financial institutions has been to squeeze the life out of the poorer countries, then they have succeeded. At the beginning of the 1990s, poor countries sent more than $4 billion each month to their creditors, solely to service the debt. If we include payments on the debt itself, this sum rises to $12.5 billion each month.[7]

In the case of Bolivia, we presently carry a debt of more than $4.3 billion.[8] Seventy percent of it was contracted between 1985 and 1999, precisely during the implementation of the NEP.[9] That is to say, neoliberalism—whether administered by the governments of the MNR (Paz Estenssoro and Sánchez de Lozada), the MIR (Paz Zamora), or the AND (Banzer)—has made us indebted more than any prior dictatorship. In 1985 the external debt equalled 51.3 percent of GNP and 33.1 percent of export earnings. By 2001, though payments fell to 21.5 percent of GNP, annual payments on the debt increased by $36.8 million as a result of interest and commissions.[10]

The debt, moreover, has noneconomic effects. The NEP has required a deep transformation of the economic, political, and social structures of the country. Everything is geared toward being "a viable country"—in other words, toward being a country that pays its external debt. Viability, for those who propagate this euphemism, is gained by enriching the banks, not from maximizing democracy or the control of social resources from below. It is gained precisely by ignoring the welfare of the population.

The external debt results first and foremost in a complete loss of sovereignty. As Bolivians, we cannot democratically decide how we want to manage our own household. The banks demand cuts in social services, for example, as a way of maintaining a balanced budget. We are similarly forced to export raw materials as a means of earning foreign currency, which results in the degradation of our natural resources. We must accept the "modernization" of labor relations—which concretely means the flexibilization of labor—because that's one of the conditions for attracting investment and receiving loans.[11]

They say that inflexible markets impede investment and development. But flexible markets produce only poverty. They say that privileging the market over workers' rights leads to greater freedom and more democracy. But the elimination of workers' rights has led only to a loss of democracy and to enormous profits for transnational corporations.

TWO YEARS UNDER BANZER

The 1997 presidential election returned former dictator Hugo Banzer to the head of the Bolivian government after an absence of fourteen years. Banzer had originally come to power in August 1971 by means of a military coup. By the time he was forced to call for elections in 1978, his authoritarian regime had tripled Bolivia's foreign debt.

During Banzer's second administration, despite his intention of rebuilding his reputation and insuring his legacy, the quality of life for ordinary Bolivians plummeted. The economic crisis that continued to develop during the Banzer government set the stage for the Water War.

Until 1997, manufacturing capacity in Cochabamba was utilized at an average rate of 60 to 70 percent. By 1999, it barely functioned at 48 percent of capacity, which meant there were massive job losses. Some officers from the local labor office even admitted that during the first half of the Banzer administration thirty workers per day lost their jobs. That was just in the formal sector, where names appeared on payroll lists and could be reliably counted. This figure does not include manufacturing's "invisible" sector, the hundreds of footwear and clothing workshops in the region, which laid off thousands of additional men, women, and children.

The tens of thousands of unemployed workers had come to constitute an important reserve army of people who were willing to work in less than human conditions. This development seriously affected workers who were still lucky enough to hold onto their jobs. Job security became so precarious that the omnipotence of the bosses and prevailing circumstances transformed the *Ley General Trabajo* (General Law on Labor), which set a relatively just standard of protection and benefits for workers, into a dead letter. Thousands and thousands of people survived in the factories each day in extremely insecure and abusive conditions.

Transnational industries continued to take over Bolivian resources. Despite the Banzer government's campaign promise to review the privatization policy of Gonzalo Sánchez de Lozada's first term (1993–1997), this did not happen. Instead, the little remaining national patrimony continued to be handed over to transnational capital. The Bolivian state turned itself, quite simply, into a servant of big capital, allowing it complete freedom to explore, exploit, market, and profit from its Bolivian holdings.

Not content to privatize Bolivia's future, the government directly engaged in illegal activities. If there was one thing that the Banzer government and its allies accomplished, it was to muscle in on, and to take over for themselves, the lucrative traffic in contraband meat that moves along the Cochabamba-Chimoré highway. Corruption in the municipal governments and the customs houses—not to mention the alleged ties to the Italian mafia—were clear signs that the true criminals could be found at the highest levels of government and business. This impunity—so characteristic of neoliberalism itself—clearly demonstrated that the ideological basis, as well as the roots, of corruption existed within the system.

The increased repression of dissent and the attempts to squelch protest that have accompanied the introduction of neoliberalism are an indication of its failure. DS 21060 required martial law;

Law 1008, which targeted small coca producers, resulted in deaths, injuries, and imprisonments; and the recently overturned Law on Citizen Security, which banned calling for blockades and protests, all provide concrete evidence that state and business administrators felt incapable of peacefully imposing neoliberalism. They had no other recourse to silence the hungry, protect the political and economic elite, or to control the population.

POLITICAL REPRESENTATION IN THE AGE OF PRIVATIZATION

The current democracy, which the country has lived under since 1982, has, in the final analysis, resulted only in the rise of a handful of politicking businessmen who raided the state treasury for their personal benefit. On October 10, 1982—with blood, sacrifice, torture, exile, persecutions, and imprisonments—Bolivian workers reconquered democracy after a long night of military governments. However, the period of renewed democracy has coincided almost exactly with the advent and implementation of neoliberalism in Bolivia. Today, more than ever, it is important to assess our experience of this democracy.

In contrast to historical periods in which unionization was prohibited, the right to assembly denied, and the press permanently censored, some things have become easier for workers during these years. Nevertheless, things have not become simple either.

Today, under democracy, organizing workers is no longer prohibited. But it is still extremely difficult to organize and to unionize because the government pursues policies aimed at disorganizing workers and destabilizing existing workers' organizations. DS 21060 opened the attack on unions and, in dismantling COMIBOL, dealt a serious blow. Article 55 has destabilized the workplace by giving bosses the right to replace striking workers and hire people for three months at a time without providing benefits. Such measures are the basis for the weakening of the unions and the cause of powerlessness of those who are bearing the brunt of the economic crisis.

There are a large number of short-term contract or flexibilized workers who are defenseless and unorganized because the unions, reeling from attack and not knowing how to address the new economic order, pay them no attention. This is compounded by the lack of a union leadership that genuinely represents workers and fights tirelessly for their social and political demands.

¡COCHABAMBA!

After nineteen long years we have come to view with great preoccupation how the Bolivian state, even under democracy, has been the force that has most aggressively destroyed, disorganized, and corrupted the union leaderships. The state has turned the overwhelming majority of union officials into its servants. The result has been pervasive distrust among the rank and file—and the atomization, fragmentation, and individualism of the social struggles and labor actions that have occurred during this time.

Political organizing similarly is not prohibited. Under democracy we are not banned from attending meetings or for organizing gatherings even if they have a political character. Nevertheless, the largest meetings, such as demonstrations or protests in which workers express their disagreement with the plans and impositions of the government, have been violently repressed many times. Leaders have been arrested, and people have been attacked and beaten by the police. In Villa Tunari in Chapare, where the *cocalareos* are based and military repression is at its highest, it is easy to recall the mobilizations, the killings, the decrees of martial law, and the confinements of people to the most remote places of the country. All of this has happened under democracy.

In 2002, the Senate went so far as to modify the existing penal code so that those who peacefully engage in highway or road blockades can be sentenced to two to eight years in prison and those accused of any type of violence are subject to three to twelve years in prison. (These changes, due to popular pressure, were reversed in 2003.) Labor organizing and social struggle are being criminalized just as they were under the military dictatorship.

If it is true that the barbarities—including torture and "disappearings"—that took place under military rule no longer occur, the police and state security agencies still have an arrogant and abusive attitude toward popular movements and labor on the whole. It is worrisome that, in the name of public security, some people have been asking that more power be given to the police. If the police are experts in anything, it is in the repression of the people, injuring the humble, robbing the workers, and exclusively serving and protecting the rich.

Another great security problem—petty crime—is impossible to consider without subjecting to severe criticism and analysis the government policies that, in fact, cause generalized poverty, personal instability, and the desperate lack of a future. The problem of delinquency can only be solved with more jobs, not more police.

How, then, are ordinary working people represented politically in the age of neoliberal privatization? The working class currently finds itself dispersed both physically and politically. Bolivian workers today articulate demands that are no longer simply demands for higher wages, because they know that higher wages on their own will not solve the dramatic social crisis afflicting our families. In general, individual workers relate to this or that political party, not in terms of activism and militancy, but in terms of what they think they can get from it. That is to say, ordinary working people participate in the electoral market to see who may be offering them a certain advantage or benefit—but that is the extent of it. They feel little or nothing about belonging to a political party, and they have no faith or conviction in the promises or programs of the distinct parties and candidates.

What is happening more and more today is that *democracy is becoming confused with elections*. At one time democracy—at least to us—meant participation in the distribution of wealth; collective decision-making on issues that affect us all; and pressure and mobilization in order to influence state policies. Now the only acceptable meaning of "democracy" seems to be *competition in the electoral market*.

This kind of politics is the official politics of the bosses, the politicians, and the foreign institutions such as the World Bank and the International Monetary Fund (IMF). These groups want their politics to be the only legitimate kind. They do their utmost to discredit our mobilizations, to dismiss our proposals, and to ignore our needs. All that they recognize as politically "legitimate" is participation in the electoral marketplace—which is a place where we are not represented and where they will always win.

Thus the working class has had to learn to represent itself politically. But it is important to specify: *through what kind of politics?* For ordinary Bolivian working people, politics can no longer mean the useless, mercantile competition for votes. Instead, we must see ourselves as engaged in politics every time we demand our rights. We perform politics when we block the bosses from laying off more workers. We practice politics when we broaden and build our unions. We carry out politics when we criticize and debate the most important issues on the public agenda with the bosses and the politicians. And we engage in politics when we fight together to defend our social patrimony.

More than anything, we are learning to politically represent ourselves by advancing and pursuing proposals of our own—*by inspiring ourselves to say how we want things to be and then to fight for that vision.* And we will not win those things by electing a worker to the city council, or by disguising ourselves as congressional representatives. We will only win a better world through day to day struggle—in the resistance against the arbitrariness of the bosses, in learning about and developing ties with workers in other workplaces, in educating ourselves in the union schools so we can figure out what we want and how to get it.

This leads us to realize that our participation in national politics should not be reduced to the few seconds it takes to deposit our votes in a ballot box. Marches, protests, road blockades, and building occupations are neither adventurous lunacy nor destabilizing conspiracies against democracy. They are simply actions available to ordinary people, to those of us who comprise the *pueblo.* Our struggle, and our duty, is to continue to advance in the project of defending our lives, our families, our *compañeros,* and our nation against the handful of pillagers of democracy. Yesterday these robbers were dictators. Today they disguise themselves as democrats who promise to create five hundred thousand new jobs and to fight poverty. At the end of the day, however, their strategy for eliminating poverty is to eliminate the poor.

For us, politics is not the electoral market. Politics should mean the collective discussion, decision-making, and implementation of solutions for our common problems. In Cochabamba one common problem was water.

ENDNOTES

1. DS 21060 contained 170 articles was passed by Victor Paz Estenssoro on August 29, 1985. This legislation is considered the beginning of the neoliberal economic model in Bolivia. Legislative acts implemented by the executive branch are called *Decretos Supremo* (DS; Supreme Decrees) and have five digits; those passed by congress are known as Laws and have four.

2. The Misicuni Project is a long-standing project to bring additional water into the Cochabamba Valley by channeling it through the surrounding hills. It is a multiphased endeavor that includes the following: construction of a dam 300-feet high; construction of a tunnel approximately 12 miles long and 11 feet wide to carry water through the hills; construction of a hydroelectric power plant to generate electricity for Cochabamba and for irrigation in neighboring farmlands; construction of new water treatment facilities; and expansion of Cochabamba's water collection and distribution systems.

3. Executive Summary, *Public Expenditure Review*, (DC: World Bank, 1999).

4. As part of the struggle to regain control of the water company from *Aguas del Tunari* and to protest the rate increase many people brought their water bills to the offices of the *Coordinadora*. During the protests large stacks of the water bills were symbolically burned in front of the *Aguas del Tunari* offices. Some of the remaining bills, which document the rate increases with analysis, can be accessed on the Democracy Center's website. (http://www.democracyctr.org/bechtel/waterbills/index.htm)

5. "The State responds [to the mining crisis] with the silence of a foreigner who speaks another language and who ignores the signs of the internal pact that had characterized the historical labor movement and the nationalist state from 1952 to 1985. The state that responds is not the politician who becomes involved according to the degree of the constituent's influence. The state that responds is the impersonal businessman who is counting his money while he is padlocking the holes [mines]."
Álvaro García Linera, *La Condición Obrera: Estructuras Materiales y Simbólicas del Proletariado de la Minería Mediana (1950-1999)*, (La Paz: Muela del Diablo, 2001), 109.

6. Pedro Rubin de Celis Rojas, *La Gran Chalada de Huanuni y Vinto*, (La Paz: Fondo Editorial de los Diputados, 2001), 135–146.

7. Gregorio Iriarte, *Análisis Crítico de la Realidad*, (Cochabamba: Kipus, 2004), 119.

8. Iriarte, *Análisis Crítico de la Realidad*, 383.

9. Victor Hugo Ayala, *Quince Años de Reformas Estructurales, Banco Central de Bolivia*, (La Paz: UDAPE, 2002).

10. *Deuda Externa Asfixia Soberanía Economica de Bolivia*, http://www.cedla.org/noticias-Deuda_externa.html

11. Flexibilization is discussed in detail in "The New World of Labor" which begins on page 107. Flexibilization is characterized by changes

including the loss of older established rights, such as job security and the eight-hour day; the increase in short-term contracted labor; the growing fragmentation of conditions in which production activities take place; and the uncertainty and insecurity of employment.

ORGANIZATION

In retrospect, organizing for the Water War began five years before the privatization of Cochabamba's water. When we started, water was not yet an issue on our horizon. In a real sense the *Coordinadora* began with an effort to reconstruct a social network, or the social fabric of solidarity, that had been destroyed by neoliberalism.

Several of us union leaders in the *Fabriles* (Cochabamba Federation of Factory Workers) had initiated a project involving both small and large unions as a way of addressing the problems of contemporary unionism. The idea was to learn about the workplace realities faced not so much by organized workers as by laborers in the invisible sector. We wanted to study the new world of work that was hardly seen or known. Out of this project a series of actions in the form of citizen proposals emerged. In support of these proposals we went out onto the street corners wearing our neckerchiefs to identify ourselves and sought to speak openly with people. We also used the media to reach people.

This outreach made it possible for many people who were not organized, and even many who did not necessarily work in a factory setting, to connect with the *Fabriles*. Our office was on the main square and this made it easy for people to come around. Women and underage workers made up some 80 percent of workers in Cochabamba. So we directed all of our attention to seeing what was going on in their world. We began to discover that there existed an invisible world of work in which conditions were truly awful. These workers had no hope and no basic rights with respect to their hours, wages, or job security.

Our first step was to try to scratch beneath the surface of this world. Interestingly, in the factories we believed that we already knew our own world of labor, but even here we started to see that there existed a world of work parallel to ours. There existed a world populated mainly by young workers, whom we had looked at as adversaries and competitors.

The next step we took was to try to make visible the new world of work. Many people in the media provided a lot of help. Reporters are constantly hiring themselves out to different publications—selling their services almost on a freelance basis. To survive, they also have to sell advertising spots on the radio; they have to design and to write promotions. The majority of workers in the media—some 70 percent—experience highly precarious working conditions. Because of this, I think, some of the journalists identified their own situation with the new world of work they were writing about.

The third step followed naturally. We said, "Well, if there exists this invisible world of work, what should we do? Not just study it and expose it. We have to organize, we have to strengthen organization, and we have to strengthen alliances." Practice and experience showed us the way forward, and so we began to organize. In this way, the *Fabriles* quickly became a kind of reference point for people. Everybody came around seeking solutions to their problems.

I remember once that a group of ex-employees of DIRECO, office workers who belonged to the administrative organization that regulated coca growing, appeared in our office.[1] They had been fired under orders from the US ambassador. So they came to us and said, "The only place we can go is to you. They've thrown us out, and we want a hunger strike in front of the US embassy because they haven't paid us the unemployment benefits they owe us." We offered our support, but it was very difficult for us because the *cocaleros* (coca growers), who were our allies, viewed them as oppressors. But, at the same time, they were workers whose rights had been violated. And by the US no less!

As the years went by, groups of people came to know the *Fabriles* and our effort to see the big picture of working conditions in our area. One day a group of irrigation farmers—peasants—surprised us. They said, "You guys are good guys; we see you out talking all the time with people. But there's a fundamental right that is being taken from us, and that's the right to water—the right to have access to water. There's a new law controlling drinking water, and that's what we want to denounce." This occurred at the end of October 1999. The peasants told us, "Broaden your horizon to defend the right to life." What they had to say moved us deeply.

During this time we were tangentially involved with a group called *Pueblo en Marcha* (People on the Move). This group was composed of professionals—environmentalists, architects, economists, and some elected officials—who stood in Cochabamba's main plaza every Tuesday to draw attention to a concrete issue. They would stick with this issue for a certain length of time, like a month or so.

For example, *Pueblo en Marcha* might put up boards with the names of all of the politicians and authorities, indicate how each had voted on the selected issue, and then decide which politicians were the most corrupt. Once they brought fishing poles and set up little dolls with the names of corrupt politicians, and passersby would try to hook a corrupt official and win a prize. It was a highly innovative form of protest—a means of making contact with people who might not be willing to discuss it in a meeting on the plaza, but who might later discuss the issue in the beauty salon or on the bus.

Many members who belonged to *Pueblo en Marcha* also belonged to a larger and more influential organization known as the *Comité de Defensa del Agua y la Economía Familiar* (CODAEC; Committee in Defense of Water and the Family Economy). In early November 1999 the irrigation farmers, many of whom had organized a strong road blockade on November 4 and 5 to protest the new water law, called a meeting for November 12. It was a broad-based call, and there we formed the *Coordinadora*. During the assembly, one peasant *compañero* said, "Let's not have just 'water' in our name, but 'life' as well, because they are taking everything away from us. All that's left to us is the water and the air." And so we became the *Coordinadora de Defensa del Agua y de la Vida* (Coalition in Defense of Water and Life).

Since the *Fabriles* already possessed a more or less adequate infrastructure—meeting rooms, internet service, a fax machine, telephones, and a space where people could gather informally—

we proposed that the *Coordinadora* should function out of the *Fabriles* office.

In this way we began to sponsor informational and organizational meetings and, in short, became much more involved in the water struggle, even though at that time we did not understand the issue very well. It was only after the *compañeros* from *Pueblo en Marcha* led a very large meeting at the *Fabriles* office that we truly understood. They explained the water law in detail and how our systems in the workers' neighborhoods would be affected, especially by rate hikes and confiscations.

THE COORDINADORA

The formation of the *Coordinadora* responded to a political vacuum, uniting peasants, environmental groups, teachers, and blue- and white-collar workers in the manufacturing sector. The *Coordinadora* emerged from the ordinary inhabitants of both town and country who, from an elemental sense of the need to defend such basic rights as access to water, called upon the whole population to join in the struggle. This call was based on understanding the importance of joint actions and believing that no individual sector alone could marshal sufficient strength to block the privatization of water. There could be no individual salvation. Social well-being would be achieved for everyone, or for no one at all.

The *Coordinadora* initially represented mainly peasant farmers, irrigators, local water committees, and urban neighborhood water cooperatives. The water cooperatives consisted of people who were not linked to the main water system but who had built autonomous systems created by sinking their own wells. The *Coordinadora* soon grew to include people who were connected to the central public water mains, but who felt that the new rates were inflated, abusive, and unaffordable. The *Coordinadora* also involved unionized workers, primarily on an individual basis or those associated with the *Fabriles,* who, because of their experience in labor struggles, contributed crucial tactics during the times of fiercest conflict.

The *Coordinadora* spoke in the name of people who felt ignored, excluded, and neglected. It spoke in the name of those who, prior to the so-called Water War, could find no space within which to voice their ideas, to express their suffering and hope, or to debate solutions to the harsh realities of their everyday lives. The *Coordi-*

nadora became, in fact, the "conscience of the people"—a living, breathing force that monitored and challenged the actions of government and big business alike. It became the organ that could interpret and decipher the basic demands of the population.

We discovered in the *Coordinadora* that meetings, assemblies, and barricades were the main instruments for struggle and liberation. Through these activities and events, we learned not only that we could reclaim our dignity and recover our voices, but also that the impoverished conditions of our existence resulted from, among other things, the huge and shameless theft known as privatization. Thus the *Coordinadora* became a place where humble and simple people—ordinary working people—proved that by organizing, and by creating solidarity and mutual trust, people can lose their sense of fear and give a real content to democracy. Only in this way could we regain what was ours. Only in this way could we seek to transform our own situation, our own reality.

In simple terms, democracy for us answered—and still answers—the question who decides what? A tiny minority of politicians and businesspeople, or we ourselves, the ordinary working people? In the case of Cochabamba's water, we wanted to make our own decisions. That was what democracy would mean in practice, and that was what the *Coordinadora* set out to accomplish.

MOVING INTO ACTION

Out of the November 4 and 5 roadblocks organized by the irrigators emerged the Civic Committee. Chiefly composed of the mayor and representatives of the local elite, its members had played a role in facilitating the contract with *Aguas del Tunari*. Thus, despite their attempt to play an intermediary role in the face of popular discontent, we did not trust them. At the meeting which founded the *Coordinadora,* we refused to recognize the Civic Committee.

As the "head of household" (executive secretary) in the *Fabriles,* I started to lead meetings and assemblies, and, as circumstances would have it, ended up as the principal spokesperson for our resolutions and as our representative at various convocations. I also wrote most of our public statements and press releases. We tried to get the COD to serve as the principal spokesperson of our new organization, but—I don't know why—they steered clear of it. I think their reluctance had to do with political instructions from the top; COD leaders saw the issue as too complicated.

So we began to speak and to denounce everything the government was doing with water. We soon called our first mobilization of both urban and rural workers for December 1. The idea was to launch a campaign around a common problem that had divided us in the past. Forty percent of the water consumed in Cochabamba came from irrigation wells. The interests of city dwellers and country dwellers had often been opposed to each other as an increased supply of city water came at the expense of water for the farmers and vice versa. Hence, we did not think it would be a huge demonstration. Even the *cocaleros,* the organization of coca growers, had said, "Why should we bring people? What are we going to do at this thing?"

But the response of the people surprised us: ten thousand people showed up! Neighborhood water committees, irrigators, people from the suburbs and the city, people who didn't usually respond to calls from the traditional labor movement—they all started to believe in us. But more than believing in us, they began to believe in *something*—in an ideal, in the fact that somebody was telling the truth and not lying to them. This ideal especially stood out in the context of the municipal elections, in which everyone knew the politicians were deceiving us.

The politicians objected that we were out to discredit candidates in city-wide elections. After the elections, however, we continued to speak out and people started to believe our denunciations.

The turnout at the demonstration was larger than at any of the candidates' election rallies. This inspired us. The protest evolved into an open town meeting at which we decided to give the government until January 11 to tear up the contract with *Aguas del Tunari,* to repeal the water law, and to reverse the rate hikes. We also pledged that, if the government did not respond, we would initiate an indefinite blockade of regional highways and roads.

In order to gain a political space for themselves, the Civic Committee also mobilized for January 11 by calling for a citizens' strike. With the support of the transportation workers who responded to the Civic Committee's call, both the strike and our blockades were successful. But, as it turned out, their strike was a twenty-four-hour affair, while our roadblocks were meant to be indefinite. This became our first trial by fire. On January 12 we had to maintain the blockades by ourselves, when the transportation workers returned to running their buses and trucks, businesses reopened and the factories resumed production. We realized then that only in the rural areas had workers responded well. A problem existed in the city center.

Nonetheless, I vividly recall a promising episode that took place the same day as the citizen's strike. The bosses had fired sixty workers from my union at the MANACO shoe factory. We held a meeting the morning of the twelfth to plan our response. We decided to hold a twenty-four-hour strike in support of the fired workers and, secondarily, in solidarity with the road blockades. Our strike would also commemorate the struggle of the old MANACO workers, because the union had been founded on January 12, 1944. In other words, all these events converged on our union's anniversary.

The MANACO factory is located in Quillacollo, 13 kilometers outside the city center. A significant quantity of the water consumed by Cochabambinos originates in this area. As part of our strike, five hundred of us workers rode bicycles from Quillacollo to downtown Cochabamba. We rode down to tell them they should stop work and continue the water protest—that the water provided from Quillacollo was water they should defend—because they would be the ones most affected by the privatization of water.

To convey this message, we snarled traffic. When drivers got mad, workers busted car windows and forced shops to close. Then we held a town meeting in the plaza and decided that the government should send a commission to discuss the water issue with us. The city was paralyzed again.

The next day—January 13—the government showed its disrespect for us. They had asked us to meet their commission at a specific time, but they arrived hours late and this infuriated the people gathered in the plaza. While we were negotiating, the police began gassing the crowd. Evo Morales, of the *cocaleros*, and I left the meeting shouting that we could not negotiate if the people were being repressed.[2] But the police persisted with the repression. For the first time in twenty years, I smelled—many Cochabambinos smelled—tear gas. The last time we suffered a repression like this was in 1982, when a massacre of factory workers had occurred in the plaza.

Later that day we succeeded in getting the government to sign an agreement in which they promised to revise the privatization contract and the water law. The government refused, however, to reconsider the rate hikes. This was a grave omission because the rates were a sensitive issue. So we presented the agreement to the people to consider and they expressed a good amount of disagreement. They began to shout, "We don't have to pay," and, in effect, the assembly concluded that no one should pay. And the people didn't pay—they resisted. They brought their water bills instead to the *Coordinadora*. This was a very important act because it signified their belief in us and we added great symbolism to it by burning stacks of bills in the main plaza.

The agreement gave the government three months to respond to all the points we had raised. But we thought that we should organize another assembly in the meantime in order to evaluate the agreement. We also thought that we needed to stage another mobilization in order to let the government know we were not asleep. This time we planned a completely peaceful demonstration—without road blockades—for February 4, 2000. We called it *la toma de Cochabamba* (the takeover of Cochabamba).

ENDNOTES

1. DIRECO *(Dirección Regional de la Coca)* is the regional organization designed to interdict coca production. They are the main body involved in the persecution and repression of coca farmers.
2. Evo Morales is the main leader of the *cocaleros* in Bolivia and the president of the political party *Movimiento al Socialismo* (MAS; Movement Toward Socialism). He finished second in the presidential elections held in 2002.

WAR

All the talk about taking over Cochabamba frightened many people—businessmen, state officials, city council members—and they said things like "the Indians are coming to seize the city." We did call it the takeover of Cochabamba, but we meant it in a symbolic way. We said we were coming to *take* what is ours—the main plaza—to *take* it over physically and in a peaceful way. We were coming to *take* each other by the hand—workers in the city and workers from the countryside—and we were coming to *take* our own decisions. That is why we called it *la toma* (the takeover).

But the bosses and politicians did not believe that we intended to be peaceful and said, "No, you're deceiving us." They asked for guarantees, for soldiers to safeguard the streets. Days before the event, *Grupo Especial de Seguridad* (GES; Special Security Forces) were deployed throughout the city in strategic locations. The GES sought to block the arrival of peasants from Parotani, Tolata, and other areas. The famous *dálmatas* (dalmatians) from La Paz—the police who are called that because of the way their uniforms look—also arrived on their motorcycles a few days ahead of time. That got on people's nerves. They shouted, as if to say nothing big is going to happen, "Get the *dálmatas* out of here!"

The national minister for government showed up, along with the information minister and I don't know how many other ministers, congressional deputies, and senators. They asked us not to go ahead with the takeover. And we said, "Nothing's going to happen, it's a *toma* with white kerchiefs, with flowers, with musical groups"—and in fact we had hired a band—"it's like a big celebration." But they did not believe us.

THE FEBRUARY DAYS

The repression began at nine in the morning on Friday, February 4, at the four cardinal points of the city, where different columns of marchers had massed. The soldiers did not allow us to move even 200 meters before they started firing tear gas and using their clubs. People outmaneuvered them in key zones, however, and we were able to advance to within two blocks of the plaza. As the police retreated from that area, we saw how the downtown residents, who had been watching from their windows, began to identify with the protestors from the countryside. The protestors cried, "We're fighting for you. Your water rates have risen. Come and join us in the streets!"

One incident stands out in my memory as an example of this. We were trying to escape from the tear gas and we knocked on a door to ask for a little water. With great fear a whole family opened their home, and a group of us went in. We told them why we were fighting: "For control of the water system. They've raised your rates, too. We have to get out and fight them—it's the only way." Back in the streets, a little while later we noticed that all of the family members were there with buckets of water from which people could drink or wash off the tear gas. Soon after that, we saw the whole family on the street corner where the worst of the fighting happened. There they were—with baking soda painted on their faces, with bandanas soaked in vinegar, with rocks, with everything. They had joined the fight.

This happened all across the city. People began to involve themselves in the struggle. I remember on one corner we asked some bank employees for paper to burn. "Paper, paper!" we yelled, because burning paper helps to reduce the effect of the gases. And the "suits" who were watching the street action from behind closed windows opened them and began to shower us with bank stationery, computer paper, printing paper, and whole boxes of paper from the *Banco Económico*. The people shouted back, "Bravo! Long live the bank!" It was amazing how people got involved.

Friday's battle was exhausting. There were moments of ad hoc truce, when both the police and the citizens sat down or lay out on the pavement. We said to ourselves, "No one will demonstrate

tomorrow." But something had deeply wounded the people, a series of things that they felt inside and could not forget. We made
our way downtown on Saturday, February 5, thinking no one was
going to show up.

As we walked, however, we soon realized that the entire city
was blockaded. The citizens had armed themselves with bricks
and stones, and television cameras were broadcasting everything
live. People watching at home responded, saying "This can't be,"
and they marched out to join in. We had guessed that nothing
would happen that day, but then we heard ordinary people being
interviewed on the radio saying things like: "We've got to take to
the streets," "They've unleashed the *dálmatas* against us," and "We
can't let them get away with beating us." I think the press played
a huge role on Saturday, because it revealed to the populace what
was going on in the city.

The *dálmatas*—the motorcycle cops—had really upset the population, and, I think, this was the government's first big mistake.
People had hurled insults at the *dálmatas* saying, "Go to hell, you
bastards, you pricks. Go back to La Paz, you *cholos!* Let our own
police beat us, not you!"[1] People simply would not put up with La
Paz police being sent to attack Cochabambinos.

That second day people came out to demonstrate with more
strength than ever. The *cocaleros'* actions were decisive, for they
were the first to take up positions and to erect the barricades
anew. We witnessed so many interesting things. For example, on
one street—an isolated street where surely nothing was going to
happen—we saw a barricade made out of sticks and bricks all
arranged in a pattern, as if it were a game. And in the middle of it
there was a child-size bicycle. The whole structure of the barricade
emanated from it. Kids had built this!

As we passed by, the children called out to us, "Be careful,
compañero Olivera. Be careful not to puncture a tire." That's when
we noticed they had placed some shreds of paper with tacks in the
street—and this on a street that hardly anyone ever came down!

That Saturday the action unfolded mainly in the center of the
city, but everyone assigned themselves a role. The young men
were fighting the police downtown. There was a group of elderly
people—I remember this very well—on a street 300 meters away
from any of the struggle. They were out in the middle of the street

banging on pots. "We've got to do something," they told us. "We old women can't get downtown by ourselves anymore. But at least we can make some noise." And you saw kids who were five, six, seven years old carrying trunks out of their houses to put in the street, or to fill with stones. The event had become contagious, with everyone saying, "Enough!"

The agreement that was finally signed by the government on Sunday, February 6, 2000, contained something we had not expected: a freeze on the rate hikes. We gave the government two months to enact the agreement. This really gave the people a sense of strength and energy.

The greatest achievement of the February days, however, was that we lost our sense of fear. Moreover, as we left the shelter of our houses and our communities, we started to talk among ourselves, to know one another, and to regain our trust in ourselves and each other. Despite the fact that the corrupt government unleashed criminals dressed as policemen to crush us, our sticks and stones defeated the cowardly, mediocre, and corrupt government officials. Solidarity triumphed over the government plot, and we pierced through the government's cynical defense of its shady business deals.

In March 2000 we organized a *consulta popular* (popular referendum) which was the first in the country's history. More than fifty thousand people cast votes on a purely voluntary basis. This exercise of participatory democracy clearly stated that *Aguas del Tunari* had to go and that Law 2029, which enabled the privatization of our water, had to be changed.

Around the middle of March, however, we began to understand that the government had no intention of conceding anything. The congressional members had said they would consider our proposal to modify the water law, not that they would change it. And on the question of the contract with *Aguas del Tunari,* they vowed they would change nothing. In effect, the government ignored our demands. So we increased them. It was no longer enough simply to revise the contract, now *Aguas del Tunari* had to leave Cochabamba. And we wanted the water law *changed,* not considered. The government then moved to discredit us, claiming that, because of the participation of the *cocaleros* in the *Coordinadora,* we were involved in the drug trade. The government portrayed us as just a gang of vandals bent on destroying things.

THE APRIL DAYS

Two months passed and the April 4 deadline arrived with no progress. Since the government refused to act we had to. What became known as the "Last Battle" took place over the course of eight days, during which blockades cut off the main highway, and masses of protesters occupied the city center. On the final day, we would mobilize one hundred thousand people and would win the expulsion of *Aguas del Tunari*. We would also win a drastic modification of Law 2029 based on a proposal put forth by the *Coordinadora*. After fifteen years of defeats, the April days would come to represent the first victory of the people against the neo-liberal model.

But as April 4 dawned we were truly afraid. We started up the road blockades again anyway. For two days, the people answered our call with strong turnouts. But the government had learned a lesson from February: they did not bring out a single soldier or police officer. I remember people standing in the roads with bottles filled with liquid. I asked one woman what she intended to do with her bottle. "Oh," she said, "since February we've been making these bottles with water and oil." "But why?" I asked. She replied, "To throw at the *dálmatas*!" In her mind, this was to be Cochabamba's chance to get revenge against the motorcycle cops. But the *dálmatas* had not come.

We became quite worried, because it seemed that the only way to maintain our resistance was to provoke the government and get it to react. But the government kept saying, "We're not going to send out any soldiers or police. That's our final position." A popular meeting was called to discuss our response.

The popular meetings, or assemblies, contained various levels of participation. They were, on the most basic level, a space of participation of the communities. The workers came together in small assemblies according to sector—all of the irrigation farmers, for example, or the business men, or the factory workers. In this way, everybody had a chance not just to air their complaints, but also to discuss ideas and advance proposals. A space was created in which people could participate in the political process by discussing the issues and trying to reach a consensus about what the next step should be.

Next, there were the *Coordinadora* assemblies. Each small assembly of workers sent members to present the points of view of their particular sector and make proposals. These spokespeople were informal representatives who were able to speak insofar as they accurately represented their sector. People from various interest groups, such as environmentalists, intellectuals, and members of the water committees attended. Even those individuals who did not fit into one or another sector were allowed to attend these second-level assemblies, so that their concerns did not go unheard. Anyone could speak, but for you to be heard required action. There was one meeting when we were discussing whether to maintain the blockades and this group came and said that we needed to maintain them. Everyone was tired and said, "You have to talk with your action, where is your blockade?" And they did not have one. This became the first requirement to speak. It was a time for talk, but not talk without action. The *Coordinadora* assemblies were where the communiqués were written and strategic political analysis took place. The decisions made as a result of this process were presented for validation at the next level, the *cabildos* (town meetings).

Between fifty and seventy thousand people attended the *cabildos,* which were held in large public plazas. It was in this context that final decisions were made. At this level of assembly, though representatives addressed the crowds, there was an undercurrent of popular democratic participation and commentary. The crowd reponded to different proposals by expressing a collective sentiment, by either applauding or making disapproving noises such as boos or whistles. Sometimes the leaders had to follow the people.

This was the case when we were discussing how to break the stalemate with the government. Our idea, the idea we presented, was to give the government twenty-four hours to tear up the contract with *Aguas del Tunari.* But people did not want to wait for a deadline. They said, "We're going to take over *Aguas del Tunari* right now," and started to head to the office. The people had chosen, so I went too. There was much symbolic merit to tearing down the *Aguas del Tunari* sign, but I tried to remind everyone that the building itself was our collective property and destroying it did not constitute a blow against the foreign company.

¡COCHABAMBA!

I had to stand up in front of tens of thousands of people to tell them this, and to tell them that the process may be more gradual and involve more compromise than they might want. This was a very difficult thing to do, but we were trying to take care of the people so the government would not have any excuse to repress them. I remember speaking to the people, gesturing to them to calm down by making downward motions with my extended hands. Later on, the opposition used a film of this, of me calming the crowd, in an advertisement against me saying I was trying to incite the crowd to more violence. But the people responded to what I was actually saying and acted with great responsibility.

They did take *Aguas del Tunari* over, symbolically occupying the company's offices, ripping down its big sign, and everything. They did not destroy the offices because social controls existed within the crowd to guard against the kind of destruction that would be detrimental to our cause. We knew we could trust each other because we all had the same enemy. Even as this occurred, not one police officer appeared. It was really pretty strange, and we had no idea about what to do.

The next day a committee was formed to discuss our strategy. A delegation of ministers had come to Cochabamba to discuss the situation. As always, they ignored us—the *Coordinadora*—and chose to meet only with the Civic Committee. We determined to take over the prefecture, to surround both it and the police station because everybody except us—ministers, members of congress, mayors, business leaders, the Civic Committee, the unionized truck drivers—was already inside.[2]

And there we were outside, waiting at the archbishopric for the delegation to emerge. But everyone stayed inside. So we declared, "We're not moving from here as long as there's no solution, until *Aguas del Tunari* is told to leave." Since we could not possibly consider standing on the sidelines while all the decisions were being made, we went to confront those inside. We could not get in through the main door, so we had to enter through a door behind police headquarters. Once inside, we immediately ran into the vice minister for government, who told us they had no intention of dealing with us. We turned around to leave, but the protesters outside commanded, "No! You stay there. Come out when you have a signed agreement. You don't get to leave until you do."

We stayed there, in a room by ourselves. The people would not let us out, and the government would not let us in. After a while, Manfred Reyes Villa, Cochabamba's mayor at the time, tried to negotiate approval for us to attend a caucus of the Cochabambinos, consisting of the Civic Committee and others, so that those who lived in the city could arrive at a decision together. But the Cochabambinos allowed into the meeting did not represent the desires of the ordinary people. They wanted an intermediary solution; they wanted to revise the contract with *Aguas del Tunari,* not to annul it, as we wanted.

It had taken three or four hours for us to secure entrance to the caucus. When we finally succeeded in entering and proceeded to defend our position, we heard tear gas being fired. Just as we shouted, "What's going on?" the police burst into the meeting room and announced, "*Señores,* you are all under arrest." In front of ministers, businessmen, and congressmen, the police one by one called out the names of those of us from the *Coordinadora.*

We were immediately taken into custody. The police then dispersed the crowd around the prefecture and the police station. Television cameras were filming as the police made a kind of human funnel to get us over to the jail. The television cameras continued to roll as we were forced to sign a warrant that accused us of *sedition and the destruction of private property.* The charge of sedition was the government's big mistake because it galvanized the population against them.

After four hours in jail, thanks to the efforts of the archbishop they prepared to release us on bond.[3] It was 3 a.m., and we said, "We don't want to leave, because you have accused us of treason." Exactly as they had dragged us in, they threw us out—with pushes and shoves. This was another big mistake. The press was waiting, and we were able to issue a statement.

On April 4, the first day of the protest, there had been twenty thousand protesters in the main plaza. The next day, there were only five thousand, and we could see that people were getting tired. But after the police arrested us, with the members of congress there or the charges raised against us—I don't really know the exact reason—a multitude of forty thousand people gathered in the plaza to say, "This is the end of it, right now!"

We held a town meeting on the spot to discuss strategy and tactics, and it was decided that we would occupy the plaza until we had our answer and *Aguas del Tunari* was gone. That is when we were told that planeloads of soldiers were on the way. We gave instructions that, as in February, everyone should take up combat positions around the plaza, dispersing themselves throughout the neighboring blocks. People got ready all over the city.

You could see on every corner the role that each family had been assigned. Children, old folks, young men and women—all of them had their faces painted as in war. Young people wore leather gloves to hurl back the gas canisters. You saw others with gloves holding barbed wire to string on posts from one side of the street to the other. Others had bottles ready to break on the ground. Middle-aged women were ready with buckets of water to throw on the gas canisters. You saw these things on every street. And there was such a level of trust among the people that they would give their money to buy supplies for the resistance without worrying that the money would actually be used for personal gain.

People made me change my clothes, because orders had been given to assassinate me. I changed, but people still recognized me. I painted my face, with the same result. We were circulating among the people to encourage them when we were called for a meeting at 4 p.m. that afternoon. I had decided not to attend the meeting, figuring it would be just a lot of smoke, but people came up to me and said that everyone had gone in—businessmen, the mayor, the same cast of characters as always—and that we had to go in too. So they shoved me into the archbishopric—the archbishop had called the meeting. When those inside saw me enter they were horrified. You can imagine the way I looked! And when the *compañeros* saw how scared those in the meeting became, they became frightened, too. That's when the archbishop, who had tears in his eyes, informed us that various conversations with the prefect had led to the decision to break the government's contract with *Aguas del Tunari*.

Just as we were about to leave the meeting, we heard people outside shouting, "The deadline has passed. Let's take the prefecture." That was the amazing thing. Just as we were leaving, the gassing started; just as we were about to announce the victory, the battle began. Risking our hides, we stepped outside with the archbishop to tell everyone that the official decision had been made to annul the contract.

We called a popular assembly. The people grouped together in the plaza and listened to the speeches. The archbishop asked for the floor so he could communicate the decision on *Aguas del Tunari*. But the questions on the water law and of distribution to the farmers, peasants, and irrigators were still hanging. The peasants told us, "We're not going to end the road blockades." Nevertheless, we said the city should return to normal.

Naturally, the event had to finish up with a mass. Face-offs with the police continued, but a huge multitude attended the Mass in the cathedral. So we, too, changed our clothes and went to the Mass.

When we entered, people applauded. I sat down. About halfway through the Mass, a priest whispered to me, "Oscar, everything is a lie. The government has refused to approve any of it." We got very pale, and people could tell something was wrong. At the end of the Mass, people lined up to embrace us. We were advised that martial law had been declared and that we were being hunted. The cars that the government ministry had hired to take us away were right in front of the main doors, and we knew that police agents were inside the cathedral.

I headed out the back and we succeeded in outfoxing the police. I told myself, "If there's a decree of martial law, I don't think they'll look for me at my parents' place because I haven't lived there in twenty-five years." So I headed toward my mother's house. My wife had been staying in another location for her safety. That very day I had called to tell her she could return home. Now I called to tell her she should leave again.

Halfway to my parents' house a *compañero* stopped me and invited me to a *K'oa,* an Andean ritual of giving thanks to the earth.[4] While the *K'oa* was going on the government announced on television that it had refused to overturn the contract with *Aguas del Tunari*, that *Aguas del Tunari* was here to stay, and that the decision was final. At the same time as the TV broadcast, the police were searching my parents' house and the houses of the other leaders of the *Coordinadora*. I found a way to communicate with a media outlet and stated that the struggle should go on, that the blockades should be maintained, and that the people should come back out into the streets.

The next day, I had no speaking voice because of the many speeches I had given the day before. I was given some medicinal leaves to chew, and I felt a little better. I was able to locate a journalist friend, and I told him where I was. I stood about half a block from the plaza and a block and a half away from the seventh division headquarters—right between two hot spots. When my journalist friend saw me, he hugged me and began to cry. My voice was still raspy, but it sounded special too. He said, "Say something, I'm going to record you, speak!" I began to convey a message to the people that everything was OK, but that we had to keep on fighting. Later, many people from the barricades and roadblocks told me that I had begun to cry during the recording. And when they heard me, they, too, began to cry. Crying gave them greater strength, they said.

The people resisted. To obtain our victory, we had to confront not only the police, but also the army—more than one hundred people were wounded in the struggle. An army sniper killed seventeen-year-old Víctor Hugo Daza when he was walking home from work. Daza was not even part of the battle; he had just stopped to see what was happening. Daza's assassin, Captain Robinson Iriarte, who graduated from the US School of the Americas, the training center for state terrorists in Ft. Benning, Georgia, was later acquitted of any wrongdoing by a military court and reinstated in his post.

These were days of great anxiety. We held our barricades and the government continued to hold to its position of non-negotiation. The Information Minister Ronald McLean, who now works for the World Bank, claimed that the mobilization was being financed by drug trafficking. I remember a tiny nun—a Dominican nun—who replied to this charge by saying that she was "standing on the blockade in Arocagua, and I'm not a drug dealer!"

The next day, Monday, April 9, government representatives managed to contact the *Coordinadora* and summon us to a meeting. They proposed a meeting with Vice Minister Jose Orías, who later became a prefect, and we agreed to meet in the COMTECO building near the Plaza Colón. The government promised to arrange two outside observers, and they told us everything would be safe for us. I had no security detail, no bodyguards to protect me. I was informed that a man on a motorcycle, dressed in a certain way, would pick me up. The government thought I was in Vinto, 18 kilometers outside of town. But I was actually very near. I arranged a place to meet with the driver that would not compromise the place I was hiding and was picked up. As the driver—one of Orías's assistants—and I sped to the meeting, we saw a sea of people, including women and children, walking down the main avenues and streets toward the city center.

A call had gone out that Monday for people to gather in the main plaza to take their final decision. The military occupation of downtown had been broken by the young "water warriors," who now controlled the plaza. The barricades and roadblocks had been fortified—there really was no official authority in place. The politicians all went into hiding, claiming they were being sought by government police. In reality, they feared for their lives because the people were fuming with anger and wanted to hang them. Thousands and thousands of people were heading to the town center and, despite wearing a cap and a different sweater, they recognized me. "There goes *El* Oscar. *El* Oscar, watch out or they'll betray you. They won't back down, but the people are with you and the *Coordinadora*."

These were the most anguished days of my life. I was not at all afraid of the government, of their bullets. I was afraid that the people would not agree with the decisions we might take. That was my fear.

The streets were clogged with people. I told the motorcycle driver, "Let's go down some of these smaller side streets." But they were just as impassable as the main arteries. At one point I got down off the motorcycle to cross over one of the barricades, and people recognized me: "Oscar, you're OK. Don't betray us; the people are on your side." And to the driver they said, "You'd better take good care of Oscar. The government is looking for him." They did not know he was a government agent taking me to a meeting with the government. Just a block away from the meeting place, a man stopped me and said, "Be careful. I just saw Orías enter the COMTECO building. The government is in there, so watch out for yourself." He did not realize that I was going to the meeting, too.

So I spoke with the government. There were two positions represented among the officials. One was the hard line: it does not matter if there are five hundred deaths, the contract will be maintained and *Aguas del Tunari* will stay. This was the position of the technocrats—McLean and Jorge "Tuto" Quiroga.[5] A softer line, one that was open to negotiation, was held by Walter Guiteras and a few others close to Banzer. We proceeded to negotiate the departure of *Aguas del Tunari* and the modification of the water law along the lines we proposed. A special convening of the congress, with airplanes hired especially to ferry all the congresspeople to La Paz, was reluctantly called by the vice president for three days later, and the agreement was signed.

One amusing exchange happened at the signing. The press asked Orías why the government was negotiating with the *Coordinadora* if it was a movement financed by drug trafficking. He replied that, first, what government officials perceived sitting behind a desk in La Paz was one thing, and reality another. He personally had confirmed that the *Coordinadora* was not just five vandals, but rather one hundred thousand people in the streets ready to do anything. Second, he was sure that it was not a movement of drug dealers because, when he left his house during the blockade, two of his neighbors, elderly ladies, were helping to block the street. There was no way they could be involved in the drug trade.

At no point in the struggle did the *Coordinadora* fight to take charge of the municipal water company. During the negotiations the government argued that someone had to take over the company but insisted that it could not be the *Coordinadora*. And we said fine, because we had not fought to be able to run it. We all agreed that the municipal government would take charge and that the water company would revert to municipal ownership.

When we presented this idea to the people, however, they said, "We do not want the municipal government in charge. We want the *Coordinadora* to control the water company." But we could not take it over—first for technical reasons, because the *Coordinadora* was not a legally established entity and the government could not just hand it over to us; and second, because it was not what we had fought for. Eventually we found a middle ground where a transitional board of directors was constituted, consisting of two members from the *Coordinadora,* two from the mayor's office, and two from the unionized workers at the company. The mayor even went so far as to say that the city would not assume responsibility for the water company if the *Coordinadora* did not participate on the board.

And that's how it ended. We signed the agreement, the blockades were lifted in the city, and the barricades came down. We maintained the rural blockades one more day, until Congress had made the changes we wanted in the water law.

Many people think that I was not happy with the outcome. I did sort of slip out the back door after announcing the results. In February, a Trotskyist group had considered it a betrayal to have signed an agreement at the time, and that we should not have given the government a respite until April. The same thing was said in April. A lot of people said, "No. We have to raise the level of struggle. We can't abandon the peasants and irrigation farmers." I hope the decision did not abandon the peasants and irrigation farmers, but we felt we needed to accelerate reaching an agreement and demobilizing in the city because a new prefect was taking office. He was a military man with an obscure past, and there was a lot of pressure from the government to have this end very badly for the people. We could not risk peoples' lives to that extent. We have never said this publicly, but the government was looking for a pretext to carry out a massacre.

I was convinced that there was a moment when a massacre was certain if the protests continued. The government basically warned us that we had to buy time to avoid a massacre. Moreover, after eight days of fighting, people were tired. We still don't know today if it we made a good or bad decision. A lot of people thought there existed an opportunity to create a kind of autonomous government in Cochabamba, since the commander of the seventh division had withdrawn his troops after they killed Victor Hugo Daza, the prefect had resigned following the government's deceit, and the popular force had defeated all the official organs of power and decision-making. I do not know if this would have been possible. But maybe there will be a chance in the future.

I do know that never in my life have I seen so many people mobilized at once. Many older Cochabambinos said the mobilization was bigger than in 1952 during the revolution—bigger than anyone had ever seen. Our fathers, our grandfathers all told us that they had never witnessed anything like it. People from all walks of life participated. They said we had all united. There were the rich from the northern part of the city, with their clothes, their water, and their food, but this time something was different. This time they marched behind the slogans of the poor, instead of the other way around—the way it usually happens—with the poor marching behind the slogans of the rich.

WHAT VICTORY HAS MEANT

On February 16, 2000, after the second mobilization of the Cochabambinos, the *Coordinadora* issued the following statement:

> The other great achievement of this mobilization is that we lost our fear. We came out from our houses and narrow communities in order to talk with each other, to get to know each other, to learn again how to trust each other. We occupied the streets and the roads because we are their true owners. We did it with our own strength. No one paid us, no one required us to mobilize, and no one fined us. For us, the working population of the city and the countryside, this is the real meaning of democracy. We decide and we act. We debate and we set things in motion. [6]

The Water War revealed the fatigue and weariness of all Bolivians in the face of more than fifteen years of neoliberal policies imposed by the government and the organs of international finance. We were mute spectators. We watched layoffs and unemployment, the sale and denationalization of each one of our industries. Yet, in a time of privatization and monopoly, ordinary working people were able to "unprivatize" the monopoly of the word—of voice and expression—and reclaim this right for themselves. After April the local and national governing elites know that the people have recovered their memory and dignity.

We also had to "unprivatize" the very fabric of society. We discovered how difficult it was to reconstruct solidarity in a society that had been fragmented and atomized by neoliberalism.

The gradual breaking up of the labor movement under neoliberalism became starkly evident in April. Rather than the traditional labor movement, it was the new world of work that came out into the streets: the unemployed, the self-employed, the young, and the women. The MANACO workers were among the few organized unions that mobilized in February and April. Nevertheless, the *Fabriles*—which set an example of transparency and keeping one's word, which had truth on its lips and solidarity in its heart—acted as a moral reference point. The *Fabriles* articulated the despair, the anger, the needs, and the dreams of the old and the young, of men and women, of country dwellers and townspeople.

We workers were capable of demonstrating to the population the possibility of transforming our conditions of existence, of revealing a horizon of struggle and victory. We did not participate in a top-down fashion, but rather stood, from our neighborhoods and communities, shoulder to shoulder with this new world of work that neoliberalism itself has created. This new alliance, which blocked the highway, took and occupied the main plaza, and recovered our water, points the way forward.

As the April blockades were winding down, one family stopped me on their way home. "*Compañero*, now that the water is still going to be ours, what have we really gained?" a woman asked me. "My husband will still have to look for work. As a mother and wife, I will still have to go out into the street to sell things, and my children will have to drop out of school because there's just not enough money. Even if they give us the water for free, our situation still won't have gotten better. We want Banzer to leave, his ministers to go with him, and all the corrupt politicians to get out. We want social justice. We want our lives to change."

This encounter made me realize that, behind the gigantic collective struggle for our water rights, spaces had arisen—in the blockades and occupied plazas—where the people deliberated the issues that most impacted their lives. It was in these spaces that people began to know each other and to share their problems—problems which, after all, were common among all of them. They soon realized that the act of coming out of their homes and neighborhoods to occupy the streets was, at its core, a fight to improve their conditions of life. And they realized these improvements could not come under the current social and political system. They had begun to work to give a true content to democracy.

Although many of us fought in the 1970s to restore democracy, our victories were usurped by democracy's enemies. In April 2000, the content of the struggle became concrete as the search for an authentic democracy. In simple terms, it became a question of returning power to the people.

The Water War did not end with the recovery of SEMAPA (the water company) for the people. It merely indicated the horizon and set the framework of the *Coordinadora,* which is none other than the struggles in people's daily lives. That was what the *compañera's* anguished question conveyed: What have we gained?

From our struggles and investigations we have learned three things. First, it is ordinary working people who achieved justice. Second, all of our individualism, isolation, and fear evaporated into a spirit of solidarity. During the worst confrontations, there were people who brought water, who handed out food, who gave rides, who took care of communications. These are elements of a well-organized resistance. People lost their fear of the bullets; they lost their fear of repression. The ghosts of past times of terror were defeated on the blockades. The third thing we learned is that we want democracy. We want a government that takes our views into account—not the interests of the international financial institutions and their neoliberal politicians.

The apprenticeship we have gone through has shown us that it is possible to construct a country in which we can make the decisions, in which our opinions count. This would be a country in which we had our own voice, where we controlled our right to speak. It would, at last, be a country in which we were actors, not spectators.

ENDNOTES

1. A *cholo* is an indigenous person who moves to the city. In Spanish colonial times, *cholo* not only described a racial heritage but also specifically referred to a "civilized Indian." It contains the idea of one who is culturally alienated and who may have chosen to abandon their culture.
2. The prefecture is the building that houses the offices of the prefect. The prefect is a direct appointee of the President of the Republic to local government. The prefect in Cochabamba at the time of the water rebellion was Hugo Galindo.
3. The archbishop of Cochabamba is the Most Reverend Tito Solari.
4. A *K'oa* is an Andean ritual of giving thanks to the earth. The ceremony involves the burning of various leaves and incense, coupled with songs and prayers of thanksgiving.
5. Jorge Quiroga, vice president at the time, became president when President Hugo Banzer resigned for health reasons in July 2001.
6. A version of "What Victory Has Meant" was originally published in *Pulso,* December 29, 2000, 11.

¡PERSPECTIVES ON THE WATER WAR AND THE COORDINADORA!

THE COORDINADORA
ONE YEAR AFTER THE WATER WAR

Raquel Gutiérrez-Aguilar

When the *Coordinadora* was formed on November 12, 1999, no one ever dreamed it would have such a profound impact on contemporary political life.[1] On that occasion, diverse social forces in both the city and the countryside came together around a clearly identified common objective: the collective defense of water against the threat of privatization.

The struggle harkens back at least to 1995, when irrigators experienced a series of conflicts with the city-owned water company over the disposition of underground water. Despite these early conflicts, the irrigators' organization, their capacity for mobilization and vision and, above all, the clarity with which they defended their right to autonomy and internal decision-making were not fully tested until the 1999 implementation of Law 2029.

Following Law 2029 and the privatization of the water company by *Aguas del Tunari,* social sectors from both the city and the country came together and united around the defense of their ownership of water systems that they themselves had financed and built. They also organized around the defense of their autonomy in the face of the state's intention to subordinate local control of water to foreign management. In a veiled and indirect manner, the resistance to Law 2029 and the privatization of drinking water in Cochabamba raised two fundamentally political questions: Who owns basic resources? And in what form should such resources be managed? These goals and questions characterized the existence and actions of the *Coordinadora* from the outset.

RAQUEL GUTIÉRREZ-AGUILAR

THE COORDINADORA'S FORCES

The *Coordinadora de Defensa del Agua y de la Vida* (Coalition in Defense of Water and Life), or the *Coordinadora,* was initially structured around the irrigation farmers already united in various committees and irrigation associations of the lower, central, and upper valleys in the state of Cochabamba. The tightly knit irrigation farmers were well-organized and solidly opposed to Law 2029. An equally important social group in the creation of the *Coordinadora* was the professionals. They were more diffuse, but were able to influence public opinion, especially regarding the contract.

These forces succeeded in coming together through the *Fabriles* (Factory Workers Federation in Cochabamba). The *Fabriles's* ability to coordinate popular discontent, won through its constant denunciations of and actions against the poor working conditions suffered by unionized, non-unionized, and flexibilized workers throughout the urban area, enabled the union of these two sectors.

In the final months of 1999, an informational campaign sponsored by some of Cochabamba's professional schools broadcast the irregularities in the contract that awarded the water concession to *Aguas del Tunari.* The campaign also debated how to regulate water distribution and how to use and consume water as an indispensable element for life and production. The *Coordinadora's* concern about, mobilization against, and denunciation of several provisions of Law 2029 emerged through this campaign.

The ideas that surfaced in these discussions formed the backbone of the *Coordinadora's* discourse. Such ideas included the public character of water as a resource, Law 2029's unacceptable monopolistic slant, and the menace represented by converting water into a commodity. The slogan "The Water Is Ours!" not only circulated widely throughout the population, but also established the need to discuss what a "public patrimony" means. That is, what does it mean, in practice, to claim collective resources in the face of the wave of privatizations that have been imposed on the country in recent years.

The *Coordinadora* took shape as an instance of democratic convergence, as a meeting ground of distinct voices involving various sectors and social forces—each expressing a collective discontent. Initially, it defended immediate popular interests, and it succeeded in focusing pent-up anger and social unrest. As it developed it

54

began to address some fundamental questions. It questioned the decision-making practices of Congress and the politicians, both in relation to legislation and to the concession of national resources to private interests, and the manner in which "solutions" to problems affecting the general population were being imposed from the top. The privatization of basic resources and government interference in the locally developed solutions devised by popular groups surfaced as special areas of concern.

Little by little, the slogan "The Water Is Ours," which challenged the government's arbitrary and irresponsible decision to privatize a basic resource, grew in meaning to the point where it began to express the belief that decision-making too should be a collective and democratic affair, with wide participation by the population. In this way, there gradually developed a new way of understanding and of practicing politics—of uniting around common demands, undertaking decision-making, and mobilizing.

The movement in Cochabamba differed from earlier social movements that had been structured around trade-union forms of organization, which mobilized exclusively around the rejection of specific proposals or government measures, or demanded the delivery and satisfaction of basic needs. From very early on, it placed fundamental questions of politics on the agenda. How should we decide collective issues? In what ways could we intervene and participate collectively in order to construct an inclusive notion of the "common good"? How could we sow the seeds of full autonomy in relation to the state through our proposals to regulate water?

Any notion of including the concerns of the general population in the welfare and decision-making of the state has eroded and disappeared. If anything has been broken over the course of fifteen years of neoliberalism—and the *Coordinadora* has expressed this well—it is the sense developed by the labor movement in the 1950s of belonging to a state. These "democratic" governments have become no more than vehicles for pacts and business deals, and private clubs for the political parties. In the face of this, the *Coordinadora*'s vigorously autonomous character called into question the monopoly of the political parties over decision-making. The idea of reclaiming decision-making and, through it, of recovering alienated "social wealth," runs through everything the *Coordinadora* has done and stands for. It expresses the profound debate in Cochabamba that now surrounds the exercise, mechanisms, and prerogatives of power.

THE COORDINADORA'S PRACTICE OF POLITICS

Starting in November 1999, and gathering strength through January, February, and April 2000, the *Coordinadora* developed an assembly-style and communal form of politics. This style of operating was used in everything from the meetings of various sectors to the drafting of agreements, from dealing with problems to organizing collective mobilizations. While the assembly-style gatherings and communal direction had only a weak institutional base, they exercised enormous appeal and drew large crowds. Participation in the assemblies became broader, and they expanded to the point where they gave rise to a specific form of "unification in process" among both urban and rural groups. Over the course of the year, moreover, this form of practicing politics took important steps toward consolidation.

Basic aspects of assembly-style democracy were reborn inside the *Coordinadora*. The importance of collective meetings to take decisions was recognized early on. These collective meetings evolved from assemblies to city-wide "town meetings" at the height of the April mobilization and have become a permanent trait of the *Coordinadora*'s daily practice. Empowering representatives or spokespeople, rather than institutionalized leaders, remains another fundamental characteristic of the *Coordinadora*. These representatives must accurately represent and speak to what the collective group has discussed and decided if they want to keep their positions as visible heads of the movement.

Since the Water War, the *Coordinadora* has served as an example of horizontal political participation. Socially diverse groups—from established unions to neighborhood organizations and irrigators' committees, from associations of small businessmen and market vendors to workers in small shops, rank-and-file labor groups, young people, and professionals—use the *Coordinadora* to discuss, to deliberate, to decide, and to implement collective agreements. Moreover, participants gain practical experiences with dialogue and real democracy—experiences that are very different in content and form from the governmental simulations that simply mask imposed measures and authoritarianism. The collective capacity to deliberate and to decide what is best for the population; the possibility to collectively carry out the decisions that have been taken; the opportunity to recall, to hold accountable, and to force leaders and representatives to adhere to collective decisions—these traits have configured the *Coordinadora* as a space with clear communal politics.

In organizational terms, the internal life of the *Coordinadora* oscillates among the occasional meeting of tens of thousands when important decisions need to be taken, smaller assemblies that are called frequently but not on a regular schedule, and the more or less permanent meeting of several representatives who are in charge of carrying on daily activities and maintaining the *Coordinadora's* function of facilitating popular unity and mobilization.

Perhaps the greatest weakness of the *Coordinadora* and others who practice this form of democratic, broadly participatory, assembly-style organizing is the fragility and vulnerability of the member organizations. In Cochabamba it is the urban organizations, such as the neighborhood associations, the trade unions, the craft unions, and the professional groups which are most at risk. In the midst of a gigantic sea of unsatisfied needs and unresolved problems—from employment and a future for youth to basic services and paved streets—the urban population often finds itself easy prey to contributions and clientistic control from the political parties operating through municipal governments. The mayor's office and the political parties often offer spurious pacts which provide an occasional improvement to the neighborhood as if it were a donation in exchange for the political loyalty of the inhabitants. Such behavior constitutes an undemocratic and vertical manipulation of the internal lives of social organizations. The power of the group becomes reduced to the leaders' ability to hook up with the political parties.

For their part, the trade unions find themselves numerically reduced in terms of members; weakened by the current practice of short-term and flexibilized hires, as well as by the general lack of job security; permanently on the defensive and with little capacity for mobilization; and narrowly focused on the difficult task of preserving what few labor rights remain. Their traditional structure has not succeeded in connecting with the contemporary world of labor that is fragmented among numerous workshops and centers of labor that have a high turnover rate, little or no organizing experience, and, above all, a frenetic level of internal competition expertly taken advantage of by the bosses. In the face of these challenges, workers—a large and important constituency—are more likely and able to participate in neighborhood associations than in the unions. (This is especially so because unions are generally not present, or barred from being present, in their workplaces.) Workers' participation in the neighborhood associations, like that of all urban dwellers, is vulnerable to co-optation by political parties.

In moments of intense mobilization, the various social sectors and dispersed working people succeed in using the spaces opened up by the *Coordinadora* to express their demands and discontent. People feel they are an active part of the *Coordinadora* and, in fact, shape it and give it life. However, the fragmentation and dispersion of the social fabric, as well as the obstacles presented by the political parties during periods of little protest, make it hard for the *Coordinadora* to pursue its work of consolidating, generalizing, democratizing, and naturalizing the assembly-style and communal forms of politics it has come to represent. The difficulty of maintaining an active and ongoing organization during periods of calm conspires against the participation, deliberation, and decision-making that the *Coordinadora* sponsors.

This problem has not escaped the attention of the representatives and public leaders of the *Coordinadora*. They have proposed an ambitious organizing plan, at the rank and file level, to establish drinking water committees in every neighborhood of the city. Such committees would be independent of the neighborhood associations and the political party influence that corrodes their effectiveness. Such committees could make it possible to consolidate democratic practices and participatory public spaces that would strongly embody assembly-style characteristics. For the moment, however, that remains a project waiting in the wings.[2]

THE MULTIPLE MEANINGS OF THE COORDINADORA

The *Coordinadora* has developed, through the struggles it wages, into an organization that addresses many issues and inhabits several levels of social significance. First, it has established itself as a mobilizing force for ordinary working people that has been tested under fire. Beyond its mobilizing capacity, the *Coordinadora* is a public space of expression—a space in which to discuss common problems, to elaborate immediate demands (that usually concern basic necessities), and to plan relevant protests and mobilizations. In this sense, the organizational objectives intially identified—consolidation of the social self-management of drinking water and irrigation; elaboration of collective demands directed at the price of electricity; and preparation for a campaign to reappropriate sources of social wealth that have fallen victim to privatization and capitalization—are the expression of a generalized demand by the people for better living conditions and of their willingness to mobilize and work together around that demand.

The *Coordinadora* is perceived as an instrument of popular self-unification, and that is the only reason why the ordinary population responds with such a multitudinous presence to its calls. The participation it receives shows the confidence that citizens have in it as well as their understanding of it as a tool for action and collective protest.

From the April victory in the Water War onward, the *Coordinadora* has been converted into an example that promotes a different kind of social management from that of a traditional public enterprise. The influence and responsibility the *Coordinadora* gained after the Water War in the municipal drinking water and sewer company (SEMAPA) offers the challenge to respond to a tremendously timely question: What should be done with a de-privatized enterprise?

This is the situation that the *Coordinadora* has confronted since April 2000, when *Aguas del Tunari* was expelled from Cochabamba. As part of the resolution to the Water War, a general manager named by and accountable to the *Coordinadora* was appointed. The *Coordinadora* also facilitated the participation of a union member and two representatives of professional organizations in the executive board. To a certain extent, things with SEMAPA went back to the status quo; SEMAPA remained the municipal water company subject to some influence from the mayor's office. Nevertheless, the legitimacy of the *Coordinadora,* and its evident leadership role during the struggle to regain public control of water in Cochabamba, opened up a space of broad influence for it, based primarily on citizen support and the generalized perception that the water company had been "recovered" from transnational hands.

A series of themes have since emerged in public discussion. People have asked, "How can we expand the sense of public ownership that citizens feel about the water company beyond just the legal preservation of SEMAPA as a city-owned business?" This theme is widely discussed in terms of the character of "social property." Current law, however, allows no room for social property and only recognizes classical forms of ownership: public or private, each with its variants (state, municipal, cooperative, corporate, individual).

Substantial discussion occurred in which citizens sought to discern mechanisms that might indeed provide for a kind of social ownership, in which shares would be distributed among the total number of users and neighborhood dwellers, who would not be allowed to sell or to transfer their shares to prevent the re-concentration of shares in private hands. The idea was to organize the water company as a huge neighborhood and consumer cooperative. In the end, however, it was decided to keep the public, municipal ownership of SEMAPA, since any modification of its current legal status would have required an enormous amount of bureaucratic paperwork, including a law for the transfer of public assets.

Beyond legalities and property status, public discussion has also centered—and this is tremendously innovative and important—on the internal management of the water company and the relationship it should maintain with the population in general. In other words, the question of the *social appropriation* of SEMAPA has been placed on the agenda. This means not only its appropriation by workers but also its appropriation by its users (customers), who have an interest in being able to count on basic services. If the expulsion of *Aguas del Tunari* in effect "de-privatized" the water company, the popular will—as expressed through the *Coordinadora*—has progressed much further, to the point of insuring a real link between SEMAPA and the population, and to the point of decentralizing decision-making through incorporating mechanisms of social participation. The direction from the beginning can be summed up as the ambition to convert SEMAPA into a socially owned and self-managed enterprise in which its property form would transcend existing legal provisions in order to make room for new means of management, decision-making, citizen participation, and social control.

Despite encountering numerous difficulties, this constitutes an enormously important experience insofar as it builds an old but nonetheless very contemporary alternative which seeks to answer vital questions. Faced with the dominant tendency toward privati-

zation today, how can we give an impulse to the social reappropriation of wealth beyond the mere legal status of enterprises as state
institutions? How can we transcend classic statism, which was so
inefficient and extortionist, so rooted in immovable hierarchies
and bureaucracies, so conservative in its routines, procedures, and
mechanisms for keeping workers and the population as a whole
alienated and excluded from decision-making? How can we transform the internal processes of management and administration in
public enterprises such that they can guarantee social participation
in the most important decisions, open their books to public scru-
tiny, and permit their workers to intervene in the development and
implementation of projects and in the promotion of new criteria
for efficiency?

It is clear that at stake, once more, is the concrete manner
through which the transformation of old social practices within
the production process and management of a basic services enterprise can occur. At issue is the way to modify the ossified and
hierarchical relations of production that have characterized the
state enterprises as much as the private firms. The separation of
workers in any enterprise from the possibility of influencing and
deciding matters concerning their own working conditions, as well
as the standard practice of treating the consumers of basic services
as mere customers instead of as human beings with whom to co-
operate in order to solve the problems of providing basic services,
are social practices that Cochabambinos are little by little seeking
to erode. Such efforts are opening the door to new dimensions of
labor and civic responsibility, in which the distance between workers, technicians, and professionals is shrinking, and in which the
ordinary population is included in actions and decision-making.

The *Coordinadora* is tackling a multiplicity of concrete and immediate problems, with greater or lesser energy and with more or
fewer difficulties. These problems offer an unsurpassable space
for imagination and research into possibilities not only for resist-
ing neoliberalism but also for the social appropriation of wealth.

In Cochabamba, these themes are the object of continuous
and profound discussion within the various groups represented
by the *Coordinadora* and even within SEMAPA itself. Slowly, and
in a difficult and complex process, practical responses are being
sketched out to an infinite number of the problems and challenges

that would permit the recuperation not only of social wealth—the privatized enterprises and water—but also a collective intervention into defining the meaning of the "common good."

Since late 2000, there has been much discussion of the need to include neighborhood representatives on the executive board of SEMAPA, with the aim of guaranteeing neighborhood dwellers a voice and a mobilizing capacity in SEMAPA's internal decision-making. The weak organization of the cities, mentioned above, signifies an enormous deficiency for these efforts. The existing rank-and-file regional organizations (OTBs), which unify fourteen municipal districts, are presently undemocratic entities—they remain subject to patronage and co-optation by the local official-dom. As a result, it is necessary to develop a new organizational network, starting with the OTBs, in order to assure authentic social participation. From the position of this new network, the question of citizen representation on SEMAPA's executive board can be addressed with a much greater chance of success, since the elected members from the city's neighborhoods and outlying zones will in fact embody the expression of collective efforts to solve the problems of basic sanitation.

The *Coordinadora* has already begun to consolidate neighborhood associations that focus on basic sanitation issues. These nuclei, in the intermediate term, will serve as the pillars of the social appropriation of SEMAPA. Unfortunately, these efforts, which ought to be supported by SEMAPA, are being undertaken in the midst of continuous governmental pressure designed to discredit the water company and to throw all kinds of obstacles in its path. The debts for which payment is constantly demanded (unlike the favorable debt consolidation package offered to *Aguas del Tunari* at the time of privatization); the persistent challenges to the legal status of the water company; the haste for SEMAPA to be "regularized" by submitting to outdated laws and the controls and demands of the Office of the Superintendent of Basic Sanitation; the open intervention of the executive branch—these pressures illustrate the permanent atmosphere of government harassment that surrounds the Cochabamban experiment in the reappropriation of social wealth and the internal transformation of a public enterprise.

The discussion also remains open in relation to the internal transformation of SEMAPA—its operation, administration, and management—that ought to accompany any possibility of bringing it closer to involving the general population. It is quite clear that we are not merely talking about successfully creating a transparent, agile, and effective management, which in itself is difficult in an enterprise that has always been plagued by partisan political handling, in which many suspicions of corruption have been cast. Rather, it is a question, above all, of discovering the means through which to change the forms of bureaucratic functioning and to limit the strictly technical criteria of the company's planning and organization. This is necessary so that workers as well as the general population can make their voices heard, so that they can both influence decisions and guarantee an alternative global solution to basic sanitation in the city.

Already on the table is a proposal suggesting a possible internal reorganization of SEMAPA based on breaking with the technical-bureaucratic rationality embodied in the drastic separation of planning, carried out by management specialists, from the actual production and realization of company projects. The central idea is that independent work teams made up of technicians and operators would be jointly responsible with neighborhood basic sanitation committees, organized by the *Coordinadora,* for the implementation of multiple solutions to the public's diverse problems and needs. Such solutions would simultaneously mobilize all kinds of resources, from the neighbors' work skills, popular participation funds, and international solidarity contributions, to money from the water company itself. The company's internal relations need to be transformed in order to reduce the distance between those who bring technical knowledge and those who know the practical experiences of work. At the same time, the manner of conceiving of and linking up with the general population requires transformation. It is not a matter of mere users or customers, but of neighborhood organizations with which it is necessary to establish relations of cooperation.

Without a doubt, the plan is ambitious and difficult, but it is also extremely interesting. It embodies the possibility of opening spaces for alternative experiments that can give impulse and value to social energy in the solving of social problems. Only on the basis of audacious innovations and clarity of objectives can the goal of constructing a self-managed enterprise be achieved in a way that

RAQUEL GUTIÉRREZ-AGUILAR

outlines the main features of a new form of organizing and managing collective affairs. Under such a form, collective responsibility would not be a matter of rhetoric but rather of actual participation, social control, and common decision-making and implementation.

Finally, and very much related to this last point, another meaning of the *Coordinadora* is its capacity for politicizing a working population that has been left profoundly disorganized in the wake of the debacle of the traditional unions. This capacity includes its ability to generate spaces and mechanisms for intervening in public affairs, as well as for showing political commitment and practicing citizen responsibility via assemblies, town meetings, and mobilizations in defense of what is ours, and strongly questioning the legitimacy of government decisions. Through the *Coordinadora*, not only are the fears and indifference of wide sections of workers broken down—workers who would otherwise remain stuck in feelings of powerlessness—but also new forms of public intervention are created that go beyond, and even against, political party clientism.

Starting from ordinary working people's recuperation of their voice, of their self-confidence and trust in others, and of their belief in reconstituting their collective power, the idea of a Constituent Assembly is being generalized among the population. This Constituent Assembly would not be an assembly of experts or PhDs, but rather something that immediately concerns every citizen and every social sector. A year after the Water War, a Constituent Assembly on the horizon, along with the new experiences of the local and regional assemblies, offers the social movement grouped around the *Coordinadora* a potential for ongoing innovation and leadership. The *Coordinadora* now has a key role to play in the development of genuinely participatory political forms that transcend the mechanisms of exclusion that characterize Bolivia's weak formal democracy today.

ENDNOTES

1. Originally published as "La Coordinadora de Defensa del Agua y de la Vida: A Un Año de la Guerra del Agua," in Álvaro García et al., *Tiempos de rebelión* (La Paz: Muela del Diablo Editores, 2001).
2. The *Coordinadora* has since had success in creating new neighborhood water committees; starting with thirty there are now more than one hundred.

THE "MULTITUDE"

Álvaro García Linera

During the past fifteen years, all of the foundations that made the unions and the *Central Obrera Boliviana* (COB; Confederation of Bolivian Workers) the nucleus of urban subaltern identities have been systematically dismantled. This has nothing to do, of course, with the idea that the working class is dead, or that there are no more radical union leaders, or that the Berlin Wall came down. In reality, the social history of contemporary Bolivia is based on facts that are more powerful than any such prejudices.[1]

THE NEW MODEL OF BUSINESS DEVELOPMENT

In terms of production, Bolivia remains, as it has for decades, a geographical space where several logics of production, techniques of labor, and forms of association from different historical epochs and civilizations (capitalist, communal, peasant, domestic, and artisan) are overlaid. Bolivia also continues to be, as it has for centuries, primarily a country that exports raw materials (natural gas, oil, minerals, and soybeans). Nevertheless, it is crucial to observe how variations in relations among modern and traditional structures of production have been articulated.

Until the 1980s the dominant elites in Bolivia, in their own hybrid and delayed manner, pursued a specific set of policies that reflected the Fordist model of development that prevailed on a world scale. Development was focused on import substitution; expansion of an internal market of consumers and producers; conversion of self-sufficient peasants into property owners and wage workers; diversification of the economy through state intervention in the creation of enterprises; implementation of pay scales based on social rights; and so forth. For businessmen, politicians, opposition figures, intellectuals, and foreign financiers, on the horizon was a slow dissolution of the traditional structures of production, which they considered to be temporary vices held over from the past. They anticipated that the past would have to give way to the "modernity" of wage labor, large-scale industry, sizeable concentrations of blue-collar workers, the marketing of products and land, generalized commerce, and a cultural homogeneity based on consumerism. Bolivia's new modernity was to be regulated by a state that offered social protections at the same time as it guaranteed favorable conditions for business.

Such a model no longer works. Although the state still intervenes heavily by regulating the price of labor, insuring investments, and establishing the price of money and the amount of public savings, it has been dispossessed of its ownership and business functions. This means that it no longer takes responsibility for generating an economic surplus for exercising control over the most important and productive branches of the local capitalist economy. Today transnational capital, which has become the principal agent promoting a modern economy, controls the economic areas representing the greatest capital investment, the highest rate of profit, and the fullest articulation with the world market. [2]

The so-called "national bourgeoisie"—composed of two subbranches, one tied to the state bureaucracy and the other to the internal market—is a subaltern business sector, reduced to small commercial and artisanal activities. The export sector (mining and agribusiness), along with the financial sector (banking), have married their fortunes to foreign investment and act as its junior partner and technical servant. Foreign investment has not sought to open new areas of economic activity. Instead, it has intensively colonized the old areas built up through state intervention: petroleum, natural gas, telecommunications, electricity, transportation, railways, and banking. What is really new about all of this remodeling of the Bolivian economy is not the change in property ownership or the concentration of capital, but the change in the model in which investment is technically concentrated.

The Fordist model, known in Latin America as "import substitution," assumed a type of extensive accumulation based on the creation of large factories, compact territorial spaces that brought together many different labor processes and enormous groups of workers. Today, however, both local and foreign capital are pursuing a dispersed model of investment and employment. Production processes in general—such as those of mining, petroleum, and industry—have been fragmented into small centers of capital investment with reduced numbers of wage workers. Commerce and banking have also been decentralized. An economic model is emerging based on the fragmentation of workplaces and the atomization of people into small centers of production that are then horizontally joined with other sectors of the commercial economy.

A third new component of the emerging economic structure is seen in new forms of vertical connections between the commercial economy and the traditionally artisanal, family-based, peasant economy. Such new connections include the buying and selling of temporary labor-power because of short-term business demand; the buying and selling of labor-power in the form of semi-finished products to be integrated into industrial or commercial processes; the integration of industrial products into the peasant-communal and urban domestic-artisanal economies; increased access to money as a commodity through credit and savings; and, finally, the confiscation/expropriation by big business of the basic necessities of life (water, land, and basic services). The specific form between the two levels of Bolivia's "dualized" social structure assumed by these new relations of domination remains key for understanding the current methods ordinary working Bolivians are using to reconstitute the social fabric.

During the mid twentieth century, modernization involved the slow erosion of the traditional peasant, artisanal, and communal economies. In contrast, each sector of the national economy today—banking, industry, commerce, large privatized mining, and export agribusiness—has redeployed the collective and cultural labor systems of the peasant, artisanal, and family-domestic economies. Some effects of this change include the ability to acquire primary materials (milk, wool, soybeans, and minerals) and component parts (gold jewelry, shoes, and textiles) from small suppliers; the creation of a supply of temporary workers; the ability to depress the wages of urban workers; and the opportunity to charge higher interest rates.

To a significant degree, the neoliberal reforms of the capitalist development project have reinforced an economic structure characterized by vertical connections between small nodes of technical and organizational modernization and an extremely wide range of traditional activities, technologies, knowledge, and economic networks. In this way, neoliberalism has created a hybrid and fractal regime of accumulation that involves minimally "modernized" and "transnationalized" economic enclaves (mining, banking, petroleum, telecommunications, and cocaine) that are superimposed upon, and partially joined with (by means of extortion, domination, and exploitation), non-modern economic structures of an agrarian-communal, small peasant, artisanal, micro-business, or family-domestic variety. One could say that the model of contemporary development is a defective integration of major, formal spaces around smaller—yet dense and dominant—spaces in which labor, circulation, and consumption take place under capital.

THE RECONFIGURATION OF SOCIAL CLASSES, MODES OF POLITICAL DOMINATION, AND MODES OF RESISTANCE

These transformations in the economy have been accompanied by modifications in the technical and political composition of the popular classes. The most affected social class has been the working class.

The number of salaried workers and persons who have to work for a wage in order to earn a living is twice what it was fifteen years ago, when unionism was the axis around which the country turned. Yet the material and symbolic conditions upon which the union-form was erected, and the trajectory of the union movement itself, no longer exist.

The great enterprises and workers' citadels that forged a culture of collective identity have been replaced by numerous medium- and small-sized factories capable of extending industrial work even into the home. This has caused the social disintegration and material fragmentation of the mass of workers.[3] The fixed contract that underpinned the confident sense of the future is today an exception in the face of subcontracting, short-term work, and piecework. These new forms of contracting render collective identity precarious and promote a kind of labor nomadism limited in its ability to cement loyalties over the long term.[4] Subsequently, a weakened collective identity gives rise to what Mikhail Bakhtin terms a "hybridization" of workers' class condition and, hence, to the emergence of "contingent identities" based on workers' specific activities, their occupations, or the transitory cultural environments in which they find themselves positioned.[5] Such contingent identities, moreover, establish a dynamic of "diffuse environments" in which the space between work and nonwork is blurred.[6] The transmission of knowledge and experience through stable job categories, as well as promotion based on seniority, is also being replaced by multi-skilling, personnel rotation, and promotion based on merit and competence. All of this has the effect of shattering the function of the union as a mechanism of personal advancement, social stability, and a disciplined leadership body, and with it the old form of social mobilization based on the unions.[7]

Finally, the unions have been slowly replaced by the party system as a means of negotiation between society and the state. This has further eroded the representational efficacy the unions once possessed as political mediator and bearer of citizen interests.[8] In their place, there has been installed—in a somewhat arbitrary and unstable manner—on the one hand, an elite that endogenously reproduces itself through the private possession of the administration of public affairs, and, on the other, an immense mass of client-voters without any real capacity for intervening in the administration of the common good.

In this "dualized" environment one's sense of belonging to a community is eroding. The "feeling of belonging to a community of destiny," such as the one that the old Bolivian labor movement succeeded in expressing,[9] is being lost in the common feeling of uncertainty, absence of a collective narrative, exacerbated individualism, and fatalism in the face of "destiny."

The certainty that collective struggle is necessary in order to improve the lot of the individual is slowly giving way to a new principle of the times. Held by a majority, though not by everyone, this principle states that the better way to obtain personal benefit is make an individual accommodation with the bosses' and the government's demands. In this way, the long chain of disposition toward submission and intimidation is set in motion. Such a process interiorizes "salaried subjectivity"—the (temporary) reticence to change one's situation through joint action, through solidarity. Thus emerges a new and complex material quality of the identity and subjectivity of the contemporary worker.

This new component of workers' subjectivity spells the death of the COB—that is, of the feeling, of the conditions, and of the actual projections of workers' collective action which prevailed for some forty years. It also means the death of the union's inclusion within the body of the state. It is the death, therefore, not of unionism as such, but rather of a particular material and symbolic meaning of union, one that no longer exists and will never exist again. It is also the death of a form of workers' existence and of the labor movement—though not of the Labor Movement itself, which in future years can adopt other historical forms. The old unification of its forms, modalities, and characteristics has disappeared. To evoke or to wish for them today is a tribute to the ingenuous idealism that believes it is enough merely to announce ideas for them to become effective.

Over the last decade, we have witnessed the dissolution of the only lasting structure of national unity with a state presence ever produced by the Bolivian working class. This dissolution has opened a long period of the pulverization of the demands and collective organizations of the dominated sectors of Bolivian society. At the same time, however, it has inaugurated a slow and multiform reconstitution of working class identities, above and beyond the fragmentation. The next decade could witness the firm grounding of new historical forms of the labor movement and of working-class organization.

The dissolution of the conditions of possibility for the "union-form" has, in part, also constituted the conditions of possibility for other forms of social unification and collective action. Of course, the fragmentation of the work process, the death of the worker-official with his chain of command and organizational loyalties, and the inability of the union to act as a political mediator have demolished the form of national unification based on the workplace and state legitimacy. Nevertheless, this form has not been replaced at the national level by other structures of social affiliation with a lasting collective identity or by other mechanisms of political mediation regulated by the state. In this regard, the last decade has witnessed a regression to, or a social strengthening of, local forms of unification with a traditional character and a regional base.

THE MULTITUDE

We will not linger here over the particular circumstances that permitted the emergence of the "multitude-form" [10] during the days of social mobilization from January to September 2000—many detailed accounts already exist.[11] What we will attempt is a more structural analysis of this form of collective action—one that presents itself repeatedly in Bolivian history, although with varying characteristics in each context.

Flexible and territorial unification. To the extent that a great number of the unifications based on the workplace have been attacked by policies of labor flexibilization, subcontracting, and fragmentation of the production process, preexisting forms of territorial organization—such as neighborhood associations, local unions (peasant and craft), or professional associations—have acquired a relevance of the highest order. Formerly obscured by workplace-based unionism, the weakness of the latter has given way to a greater protagonism of these other unifying forms. It was thought that the dismantling of structures of national unification such as the COB would be followed by a long process of social disorganization—one that would be susceptible to discipline and cooptation by state-client institutions such as the political parties, NGOs, and the church. Nevertheless, the erosion of the older structures of national mobilization that could affect the state has resulted in a multifaceted, complex, and generalized organizational turn on the part of subaltern society—one that is rooted in local spaces and concerns.

One of the axes of the neoliberal strategy for reconfiguring the generation of economic surplus is that of subsuming use value to the logic of exchange value—or, what amounts to the same thing, the commercializing of the conditions for basic social reproduction (water, land, and services) that used to be regulated by a logic of public utility (whether local or state). The social wealth directly involved in this expropriation is precisely that which has a territorial function, such as land and water. This creates conditions for the practical reactivation of the old territorially-based collective social structures and, furthermore, for the production of new structures of unification emerging from the new dangers. Such is the case with the irrigator association in Cochabamba which, based in many cases on traditional knowledge and skills practiced over centuries but still adequate to contemporary needs, has created modern ways of group organization and membership in order to defend the management of water according to traditional practices and customs.[12]

Historically, these group nuclei have had an active role only at the local level because of their short time in existence, or because they have been boxed in by increasing state proscriptions against the collective political logic that guided the relationship between state and society from the 1940s on. Nevertheless, it has been the persistence, the breadth, and the collective, as well as individual, legacy of group action—not to mention the general aggression against such action by the local authorities—that have contributed to making it possible for these nodes to create an extensive network of mobilization and joint action, first at the regional, then at the provincial (county), and finally at the state level.

The *Coordinadora* is the regional and temporary name of one of the ways in which the multitude-form has manifested itself. The *Coordinadora* is, first of all, a network of communicative action, in a sense similar to the one proposed by Jürgen Habermas.[13] It is a "horizontal" network insofar as it is the result of the formation in practice of a social space of encounter among equals—namely, those affected by the social problematic of water, who have equal rights in practice of expression, intervention, and action. That is, the network is formed in and by the interactions of its members. Through complex and varied internal flows of communication, the participants in the *Coordinadora* have created a unifying discourse, a set of demands and goals, and a series of commitments to achieve their aims together. The *Coordinadora* is a network of practical action with a capacity to mobilize large sectors of society independently of the state, the church, the political parties, and the NGOs.

Unlike the "crowd"—which gathers together individuals who have no group affiliation or organizational dependence and who are united rather simply by the euphoria of immediate action—the decisive characteristic of the multitude is that it overwhelmingly represents a gathering of "collective" or collectivized individuals.

That is, the multitude is an association of associations in which each person who is present in the public act of meeting does not speak for himself or herself but rather for a local collective entity to which he or she is accountable for his or her actions, decisions, and words.

This is very important to keep in mind since, in contrast to what Habermas thinks, the power to intervene in public spaces is never equally distributed. There are people and institutions with greater discursive experience, or greater organizing ability, that enables them to influence an assembly, a town meeting, or a small meeting to incline decisions in favor of one position and to silence others. This can be observed, for example, in various strident interventions and the prearranged coalitions employed by the partisans of the political structures of the Old Left. The easy pseudo-radical interventions of these "discourse professionals" are not accountable to anyone. Their influence runs into a wall consisting of the responsibility of each participant in an assembly—in words, decisions, and commitments—toward his or her district; that is, toward those who sent them to the assembly from their neighborhood, committee, or community, and who, in the end, are the ones who accept or reject the agreements adopted in the assemblies. And these entities, in whose name the individuals act, are above all territorially-constituted organizations, in which rests a good part of the communicational infrastructure (radio stations and periodicals with local audiences, meeting places, and blockade zones) and, more than anything else, the force and range of mobilization. The multitude is not a confluence or "milling around" of disorganized individuals. On the contrary, as was the case with the COB in its time, it is an organized action of people who have been previously organized. Now, however, the forms of prior organization consist of nodes of territorial structures.

These new territorial-type organizations are the backbone that sustains the public action, the mobilizations, and the social pressure of the multitude. One of the virtues of the new territorial organizations in relation to the union-form is that they do not create a border between members and nonmembers in the way that the unions used to do. In local and state-wide meetings, in the assemblies and town meetings, in the mobilizations, blockades, or confrontations, other people—those who lack a group affiliation (individuals) or who are representatives of other forms of organization (workers' unions and ayllus)—can also intervene, express themselves, and participate. This greatly broadens the social base of action and legitimacy.

In this sense, the multitude is a fairly flexible organizational network—even loose to a certain point. It constitutes a fairly solid and permanent axis of connections. It is capable, as the COB used to do, of convoking, leading, and pulling along other organizational forms and an enormous quantity of unattached citizens who lack traditional group loyalties because of their precarious work situations and the processes of modernization and atomization. It is also a structure of mobilization that is capable of integrating within its own networks an internal dynamic of deliberation, resolution, and action, both in regard to individuals and associations, for the purpose of undertaking a search for both immediate and long-term goals.

Types of demands and the organizational base. The principal demands around which these local centers of association have begun to form have been the management of water, access to land, and the price of basic services. Together these demands delimit the space of the vital and primary forms of social wealth necessary to materially sustain social reproduction.

In the case of rural workers, the defense of their management of water and land, as well as the culture of complex social networks linked to this management, directly confronts the attempts to substitute the concrete meaning of wealth (satisfaction of needs) and its forms of direct control (familial-communal) with an abstract meaning of wealth (business profits) and modes of control distant from the users (state legislation). What is new and aggressive about this reconfiguration of the use of social wealth lies not so much in the act of commercialization, which is frequent in the peasant communities and in the *ayllus*, but rather—despite evident inequalities and internal hierarchies in the management of these resources—in that commercial value becomes not so much the expression of capital as an expression of the ability to control and regulate.

In the peasant communities, the commercialization of resources is not only governed by agreements of membership within the communal structure and the fulfillment of political and ceremonial responsibilities, but also by norms that, in greater or lesser measure, find themselves subordinated to conventions or collective agreements. These agreements themselves are founded on a different economic logic which subordinates the marketing of goods to the necessities of reproducing the community as a whole.

In the case of workers and dwellers in the cities and urban peripheries, the fight against price increases in basic services (drinking water, electricity, and transportation) concerns the defense of what could be called an indirect social wage. In contrast to the wage the worker receives from his or her employment in the form of pay or social security, this social wage, manifested through the cost of basic services, concerns the manner in which the state controls the provision of services that are indispensable for social reproduction. The first type of salary is the one that has been most affected in the last twenty years by structural reforms and the deterioration of the condition of labor. The second type is now beginning to be the object of social conflict. Insofar as this second type impacts people regardless of whether they work in a large factory or small workshop, it creates the structural possibility of a global unification of the various fragmented forces of production.

We thus find ourselves presented with the vindication of territorially-based demands because the direct use of social wealth is a result of the occupation of a specific space. We also are presented with objectives around which to mobilize. Such objectives, in areas of social wealth formerly managed according to a different economic rationality, seek to halt the advance of commercial logic and to displace the rules of capitalist accumulation.

We can use Charles Tilly's classifications—based on his studies on the transition from traditional, local structures of power to national and modern power structures in eighteenth-century Europe—to say that, given the defensive character of the needs and the local traditions comprising the social movement that arose in Cochabamba, we stand before a type of "reactive" collective action.[14] The preexistence of "local communities based on solidarity" as the platform of mobilization, and the fact that the great mobilizing force of the irrigators reclaims the vigorous cultural tradition and organizing experience of the peasant movement formed during the years 1930–1960, tend to reinforce this perspective.[15] Nevertheless, as we have explained above, the multitude-form does not only presents networks of association with a communal or traditional base; it also contains groups with an emerging affiliational base in the intermittent and mutilated processes of social modernization.

Let us clarify and develop this last idea. The *Coordinadora* takes as its molecular starting point organizational forms which can be classified as of a traditional type because many of them are founded on logics that are pre- or non-commercial with respect to access to land, water, or public services. At the same time, however, access to land or water as the focus of adherence to the movement—both on an individual and group basis—is the type of choice of object of struggle proper to modern social movements. In the so-called traditional forms of association—and insofar as individuality is a result of collectivity[16]—internal mechanisms of deliberation are based on deliberative consensus and obligatory participation. This is the case in the majority of the organizations that make up the *Coordinadora*. But the joint actions undertaken through the form of the current multitude—the coupling of the unions, irrigators' associations, and neighborhood organizations nominally integrated in the *Coordinadora*'s organizational structure—have been the fruit of a free choice outside of any force, sanction, or pressure. The *Coordinadora* has no mechanism for surveillance, control, or punishment of its component organizations. It maintains its convocation through the moral authority of its representatives, through the agreements and the persuasive arguments it brings before the regional assemblies, and through its members voluntary adhesion to collective action. In contrast to the union-form, which is the bearer of "modern" forms of conduct, the *Coordinadora* lacks a stable structure of control and mobilization of its members. It appeals above all to justice and a conviction in the cause being fought as its way of guaranteeing a mass turnout at mobilizations. The result is thus a highly ambiguous and sometimes arbitrary differentiation between the modern and the traditional. Rather, it seems generally that the social movements are simultaneously modern and traditional, defensive and offensive.

In another vein, the mobilizations of September and April 2000, as much in the *altiplano* as in Cochabamba, have used, broadened, and created public spaces in order to seek regional and national legitimacy for their demands. Through traditional but also modern techniques of communication, they have notably influenced public opinion as a way of building their base of adherents and, in specific circumstances, of persuading or obliging the governing elites to modify laws and legislation. These grand mobilizations have availed themselves of the freedoms of assembly, speech, and demonstration in order to make known the needs of their participants, to recruit new adherents, and to neutralize the state. In other words, the social movements of April and September 2000 have employed and expanded the democratic and institutional components of what is called "modern civil society." These represent civil and political rights that are not, as Jean L. Arato and Andrew Cohen show, only associated with multiparty systems, but also, and above all, represent citizens' rights that have been won by the social movements themselves—in particular by the workers' movement during the nineteenth and twentieth centuries, as much in Europe and the United States as in Bolivia.[17]

Finally, the multitude-form has also set in motion demands and actions of a "proactive" type (see Tilly). To the extent that it went about consolidating, broadening, and radicalizing the social movement, the mobilized base of the *Coordinadora* began to seek recognition for its forms of assembly-style democracy as a technique of directing civil demands and institutionalizing other forms of exercising democratic rights. These forms include the referendum of March 2000, the call for a Constituent Assembly, the direct control of political power at the state level during the days of mobilization, and the proposal to implement a form of self-management for the provision of drinking water. We witnessed a combination of the defense of resources previously owned and controlled from below (water) with the demand for resources that had previously not existed (new forms of democratic rights and the exercise of political power). All of this makes the multitude a form of mobilization that is at the same time profoundly traditional and radically modern, both defensive and offensive.

Identity. The fact that territorial formations and demands over the reproduction of the basic necessities for life are sustaining the social movement in Cochabamba—and, more slowly, the mobilizations in El Alto against increases in electricity and water rates and in favor of the creation of a public university—makes possible a new range of self-identifications. It is not the demand for access to land which is bringing individuals together, and, for this reason, peasant unionism is not the center of congregation, although unions can participate in the movement. Nor is it a demand for better wages which is causing people to join each other, and so the identity of "worker" fails to encompass the movement, even though it is involved. It is water and basic services that unite peasants, full-time workers, part-time workers, small businessmen, sweatshop workers, artisans, unemployed workers, students, housewives, and so forth. Despite their diversity in terms of occupations and cultural practices, all these groups have something in common: access to water and public services as the essential and major (since they possess scarce resources) components of the reproduction of their own lives. Whether they have access to these goods through traditional practices and customs or through modern modalities, these groups are generally composed by people who "do not live off another's labor."[18]

These constitutive and common components of the participating sectors of the mobilizations may be characterized by and subsumed within the expression "ordinary working people." This phrase plays the role of registering the movement's basis in self- or mutual recognition among equals, as its movement outward toward other social sectors. It also serves as the point of departure for laying down a collective group narrative that calls the group into being precisely as a group, as a social identity.

It is clear that identity formations are, above all, enunciations of meaning that demarcate social boundaries and that invent a sense of authenticity and otherness, with the practical effect of developing the subject thus constructed. But they are also discursive constructions that work on the basis of material supports, on facts, and in the tracks of practical action. This means that there is not an exclusive identity for the social agents involved in specific social phenomena, but neither are all identities possible. There is a broad but clearly delimited space of possible identity formations corresponding to the diverse, complex quality of the agents and their interrelationships—and it is within this space that events arise. In the case of the *Coordinadora* as a social movement, it is clear that the plebeian and laboring identity that today characterizes it might be replaced with other identities, depending on the activity of the subjects and groups that act within it. Nevertheless, the identity that has begun to consolidate itself in a vigorous manner is that of ordinary working people. This identity has proven capable of integrating local urban and rural identities, at the same time that it inherited the old national identity of the labor movement centered on the virtue of work.

WORKERS' ASCENDANCY AND THE WEALTH OF SOLIDARITY

It has been said repeatedly that in the *Coordinadora* the force of mobilization, and the collective subjects who constitute the backbone of collective action, have been and still are the irrigators' organizations.[19] It has also been said that, in practical terms, the world of flexibilized labor, and what remains of the mobilizing capacity and mass power of the old union-form, have been able to project only a diluted presence in the territorial structures of the neighborhoods, the irrigators, and the regional assemblies.

Nevertheless, there is a strong presence of labor leaders in public spaces, and, among the new nuclei of workers' leadership, there exists a critical discourse and a knowledge of the networks of power and dominance that define contemporary capitalism. There is also the experience of organization and militancy among the nuclei of unionized workers, which is the legacy of the long trajectory of the union-form.[20] There too is a material structure of workers' organization composed of buildings, publications, and organic ties with other sectors of the labor movement (neighborhood associations, small merchants, transportation workers, peasant federations, university students and professors, and professionals), which, as a whole, have been incorporated both technically and organizationally into the new social movement of the multitude.

This contribution by workers' organizations has been decisive in articulating diverse forces of discontent and diverse sets of demands. It has permitted the unification of regionalized demands and isolated efforts into a grand torrent of globalized protest. And it has contributed to the formation of mobilizing strategies and symbolic struggles embodying a breadth and impact never before seen in the history of social movements in Bolivia.

One subjective element that bears upon the moment of creating the fabric of alliances among diverse sectors has been the moral leadership of the regional labor leader. He has come to represent in his own person and political trajectory a rupture with the clientism and sinecurism of political and union life that continually spoil the autonomous actions of the subaltern classes. The fact that this kind of leader has maintained himself outside the realm of cooptation by the political parties and the marketplace of electoral loyalties has allowed the creation of a moral point of reference based on social commitment. This reference point has proven capable of awakening feelings of belief, adherence, and confidence in the autonomy of social action, in the clarity of objectives, and in the honesty of leaders.

At the end of the day, no one joins a march if they do not believe in the practical effect of the mobilization. And no one fights in association with others and for the well-being of others unless there has already been generated a "wealth of solidarity" that transforms loosely associated action into an accumulated, sought-after, rewarding, and recognized social good by the agents of social action. This wealth of solidarity is a type of symbolic capital that could—over time and through generalization—give historical continuity to the social movements. In moments such as our present circumstances, of course, there still prevails a common suspicion about the use of "solidarity" as an empty phrase opportunistically employed in political party platforms. Nevertheless, the fact that both old and new leaders and organizations with social prestige can ratify by their behavior the notion of "solidarity" as a value in itself has contributed to the consolidation of dispersed networks of solidarity and to the growing formation of a space in which solidarity is converted into a recognized and sought-after social good.

Sovereignty and social democratization. As a result of the extension of a series of local democratic practices to the state level, in addition to the fact that there exists the necessity of assuming various responsibilities of state administration eroded by the mobilization, the current multitude-form has functioned basically as a form of democracy and political sovereignty.

Having as their base, territorial structures in which assembly, deliberation, and direct consultation are daily practices for attending to geographical boundaries, justice issues, common work, police abuse, bureaucratic transactions, and even clientistic relations with political parties or the state, these extended practices of direct democracy became a support structure for consultation and the elaboration of mobilizing strategies. Starting at the regional or provincial level, the democratic know-how and techniques of deliberation had to expand as the networks of mobilization focusing on specific demands grew to the state level. In time the networks became reconfigured and gave way to a complex and systematic structure in which the public prerogatives of association, the formation of public opinions, and, eventually, resolution and execution—in this case the management of water—were democratically exercised.

Without any need to think or to desire it, the networks transformed themselves into a type of social organization that recognized no source of authority other than itself. That is, they became a government based on a structure of assembly-style, deliberative, and representative practices of democracy that de facto supplanted the system of political parties; legislative and judicial powers; and—they almost reached this point—the state monopoly over the use of public force.

Neighborhood assemblies, peasant communities, unions, and irrigators' associations; provincial and regional assemblies; state assemblies and town meetings—all of these gave rise to a hierarchized structure that combined assembly-style, deliberative democracy at each horizontal level with representative, assembly-style democracy between each vertical level. This permitted the formation of public opinion among equals at the local level (territorial assembly) and the *cabildo* (town meeting), as well as the executive condensation of opinions at the state level (assembly of local representatives, spokespersons of the *Coordinadora*).

A number of times in 2000 (February, April, and September–October), this dense web of assemblies and plebeian democratic practices not only demanded rights from the state with its system of parties and parliament, but also replaced the state as the mechanism of government, as the system of mediation, and as the culture of obedience. The multitude—and this differs from Alain Tourraine's proposal that the "new social movements" would not be political movements aimed at the conquest of power—is de facto an extreme politicization of society.[21] It possesses an organizing force capable of challenging the relevance of the prevailing systems of government—the system of liberal democracy—and of erecting (up to now provisionally) alternative systems for the exercise of political power and the conduct of legitimately democratic life.

The virtue of this social movement is that, as it has been born, it has called into question the reigning relations of domination. And to the extent that there exists a strong culture of local self-government, these logics of power and assembly-based democracy can be projected onto the state-wide or national level. In this manner it can dispute the way public affairs are enunciated, the manner in which they are carried out—or, in other words, the form of government.

Of course, this does not avoid the difficulty and ambiguity with which this appetite for political power on the part of the social movement is formed. The popular classes are accustomed to an economy run by the dominant class and to forms of moral resistance by the dominated.[22] In this pattern, resistance is governed by a logic of demands and concessions with the elites, who are confirmed as the dominant class by this very logic. The formation within the dominated of a collective spirit of permanent sovereignty is often replaced by the old habits of obedience to those who, it is supposed, are qualified to govern. On other occassions, the resistance atrophies owing to a retreat to merely local participation, thus allowing the general governance to be assumed once again by the traditional elites.

The history of the formation of a self-governing enterprise in Cochabamba is an example of the incessant confrontation between the servant and the sovereign in the interior of the individual and collective behavior of each one of the subjects involved. All in all, however, it remains clear that the subaltern classes have opened, with their own experience, a field of possibilities for the exercise of power, social democratization, and the transformation of relations of domination that may serve as a guide for subsequent actions.

Institutionalization and reach. In contrast to what was the workers' movement, the multitude-form lacks durable mechanisms of convocation and consultation that make routine the presence of a space for its components. If the local collective subjects that make up the multitude continuously maintain assembly practices, joint action as a multitude is always an uncertainty that can only be resolved in practice. From this it follows that every call to mobilization becomes at the same time a referendum on the vitality, the continuity, or the weakness of the multitude, or, in this instance, the *Coordinadora*. This reality means that an organizational culture is forged in which unity is assumed to be the result of patient work, not a given that only needs to be evoked in order to make it present, as, for example, began to happen with the COB in the last decades.

Nevertheless, this collective virtue brings with it a deficit in terms of structural presence and material continuity—that is, of organizational permanence and institutionalization—that would enable a continuous follow-up on agreed-upon tasks, the discussion of new objectives, and so forth. Thus, sometimes the *Coordinadora* consists of half a million inhabitants; at other times it can claim no more than one hundred active and permanent members. Perhaps the way of overcoming this organizational weakness is to consecrate, institutionalize, and symbolically ritualize the local and regional assemblies as institutionalized assemblies of the *Coordinadora*. This could also entail the regularizing of a state-wide assembly with a minimum of official delegates, to which others could be incorporated at any moment, and all of whom would be subject to reelection and immediate recall as delegates. Similarly, such an arrangement would require the formulation of a salary policy for delegates that would enable the representatives to carry out their functions on a full-time basis, but with better control of delegates from the base of the organization.

In this case, we would speak of a form of internal institutionalization that differs from the one set forth by Claus Offe in his model of the stages of a social movement.[23] According to Offe, institutionalization would lead to the mobilization's leaders being included in the dominant political system. Internal institutionalization, instead, would not only articulate the "expressive" and the "instrumental" functions within the same social process; it would also maintain the initial demand of social action for a radical modification of the rules and legitimate subjects of the political field so as to insure an association of equals.

Another of the difficulties that confronts the multitude-form is its regionalized character. Following the experience of the *Coordinadora* in Cochabamba, there have been efforts to construct similar instances in El Alto, Santa Cruz, Tarija, and elsewhere, that could give a national character to this form of social mobilization. The conditions of possibility for such projects are furnished by neoliberal policies themselves, which have shared out scarcity, job uncertainty, and aggression against the basic necessities of life on a national basis. To succeed in structuring local movements as a multitude and in interconnecting them on a national scale would enable a great capacity to mobilize and to affect the state. Yet, while this is taking place, it seems that in the next few years the multitude-form of the social movement will have to base itself primarily on a regional scope. The national constitution of the multitude, should it come to pass, will be the result of long and patient work, unifying trust, mutual support, leadership, and solidarity at the local level.

ENDNOTES

1. This chapter is excerpted from a longer essay entitled "Sindicato, Multitud y Communidad: Movimientos Sociales y Formas de Autonomía Política en Bolivia," published in Álvaro García et al., *Tiempos de Rebelión* (La Paz: Muela del Diablo Editores, 2001), 9-79. The pages translated here are 32-54.
2. UDAPE, *Bolivia: Prospectiva Económica y Social 2000-2010*, (La Paz: PNUD, 2000).
3. P. Rossell and B. Rojas, *Ser Productor en El Alto*, (La Paz: CEDLA, 2000).
4. Carlos Arce, "Empleo y relaciones laborales," in *Bolivia Hacia el Siglo XXI*, (La Paz: CIDES/CNR/ANC/CEDLA/CEB/PNUD, 1999). See also C. Arce, *Crisis del sindicalismo boliviano: consideraciones sobre sus determinantes materiales e ideológicas*, (La Paz: CEDLA, 2001).
5. See Homi K. Bhabha, *The Location of Culture*, (Routledge: London, 1994): Pnina Werbner and Tariq Modood, eds., *Debating Cultural Hybridity: Multicultural Identities and the Politics of Anti-Racism*, (Zed Books: London, 1996).
6. U. Beck, *Un Nuevo Mundo Feliz: La Precariedad del Trabajo en la Era de la Globalización*, (Paidos: España, 2000).
7. Á. García Linera, *Estructuras Materiales y Mentales del Proletariado Minero*, (La Paz: Comuna/Carrera de Sociología-UMSA, 2001).
8. Patricia Chávez, *Los Límites Estructurales de los Partidos de Poder Como*

Estructuras de Mediación Democrática: Acción Democrática en el Departamento de La Paz, (La Paz: Tesis de Licenciatura, Carrera de Sociología, UMSA, 2000).

9. Stéphane Beaud and Michel Pialoux, *Retour Sur la Condition Ouvrière,* (France: Fayard, 1999).

10. The concept of the "multitude-form" that we are now about to propose differs from that proposed by René Zavaleta. In general Zavaleta used this concept to refer to the proletariat as a spontaneous subject, as in "the masses in action and not as a class." On this topic see Zavaleta, "Forma Clase y Forma Multitud en el Proletariado Boliviano," in *Bolivia Hoy,* (México: Siglo XXI, 1983); also, *Las Masas en Noviembre,* (La Paz: Juventud, 1983). For our part, we will work the concept of the multitude to mean a block of collective action through which the subaltern classes give rise to autonomous, organized structures in relation to hegemonic discursive and symbolic structures. These anti-hegemonic structures may vary in origin among distinct segments of the subaltern classes.

11. Álvaro García et al., *El Retorno de la Bolivia Plebeya* (La Paz: Muela del Diablo, 2000).

12. O. Fernández, *La Relación Tierra-Agua en la Economía Campesina de Tiquipaya,* (Cochabamba: Tesis de licenciatura en economía, UMSS, 1996); G. Gerbrandy and P. Hoogendam, *Aguas y Acequias: Los Derechos del Agua y la Gestión Campesina de Riego en los Andes Bolivianos,* (La Paz: Plural, 1988); P. Hoogendam et al., eds., *Aguas y Municipios,* (La Paz: Plural, 1999).

13. J. Habermas, *Teoría de la Acción Comunicativa.* (Taurus, España: Tomo II, 1992).

14. C. Tilly, *The Rebellious Century: 1830-1930,* (Cambridge, MA: Harvard University Press, 1975).

15. J. Gordillo, *Campesinos Revolucionarios en Bolivia: Identidad, Territorio, y Sexualidad en el Valle Alto de Cochabamba, 1952-1960,* (La Paz: UMSS/ PLURAL/CERES, 1998).

16. On these constitutive forms of social individuality, see K. Marx, "Forms Which Precede Capitalist Production," *Grundrisse* (Harmondsworth, GB: Penguin, 1973), 471-479.

17. See A. Arato and J. Cohen, *Sociedad Civil y Teoría Política,* (México, D.F.: FCE, 2000). For case studies of Europe, the US, and Bolivia, see A. Giddens, *Profiles and Critiques in Social Theory,* (London: Macmillan, 1982); D. Montgomery, *El Ciudadano Trabajador: Democracia y Mercado Libre en el Siglo XIX Noretamericano* (México, D.F.: Instituto Mora, 1997); René Zavaleta, *Las Masas en Noviembre* (La Paz: Juventud, 1983);

Luis Tapia, *Turbulencias de Fin de Siglo: Estado-Nación y Democracia en Perspectiva Histórica* (La Paz: IINCIP-UMSA, 1999); and Álvaro García Linera, "Ciudadanía y Democracia en Bolivia," *Ciencia Política*, Año 4, segunda época (La Paz: IINCIP-UMSA, 1999).

18. On the concept of "people who do not live off the work of others" and its importance for the formation of collective identities among the subaltern classes of modern society, see Karl Marx, *The Civil War in France*, including its two drafts.

19. See Á. García et al., *El Retorno de la Bolivia Plebeya.*

20. Pierre Bourdieu, "Contre la Politique de Dépolitisation," in *Contrefeux,* 2 (Raisons d'Agir, France, 2001).

21. See Alain Tourraine, *Producción de la Sociedad,* (México, D.F.: UNAM-IFAL, 1995) and "An Introduction to the Study of Social Movements," *Social Research,* 52 (1985).

22. See E. P. Thompson, *Tradición, Revuelta y Conciencia de Clase,* (Barcelona: Crítica, 1979); C. Grignon and J. C. Passeron, *Lo Culto y lo Popular: Miserabilismo y Populismo en Sociología y Literatura,* (Buenos Aires: Nueva Visión, 1991).

23. C. Offe, "Reflexiones Sobre la Autotransformación Institucional de la Política de los Movimientos: Un Modelo Experimental por Etapas," in *La Gestión Política.*

DIRECTING SEMAPA
AN INTERVIEW WITH
LUIS SÁNCHEZ-GÓMEZ

Tom Lewis: What position do you hold in SEMAPA, and whom do you represent?

Luis Sánchez-Gómez: I am one of the directors of SEMAPA. I represent approximately 180,000 inhabitants living in the southern sector of the city of Cochabamba. SEMAPA has seven directors altogether: three from the population at large, two from the mayor's office, one from the professional schools, and one from the SEMAPA workers' union.

The three of us who represent the population were voted into office in free and direct elections held April 30, 2001. The regular meetings of the board of directors take place every Tuesday, with extra meetings called as needed.

TL: Why did you decide to stand for election to SEMAPA's board of directors?

LSG: The decision belonged to the various Water Committees of the southern zone of the city. They first sought to nominate the Reverand Javier Velasco, a local parish priest and the initiator of many neighborhood water projects, but after it turned out that Father Javier was moving to another city, the committees decided to nominate me—and I accepted.

Initially, I thought it would be preferable for a leader of one of the water committees to stand as a candidate. But their analysis was that the mayor's political party, the *Nueva Fuerza Republicana* (NFR; New Republican Force), was going to try everything possible to make sure that one of their members won the election. Thus they thought it would be more prudent if we fielded a candidate who had a strong chance to beat any of the mayor's possible candidates.

It turned out that this was a good decision, because the mayor's office really did try everything it could, including illegal and immoral tactics, to prevent my being elected. Besides, we ran one of the water committee leaders (Raúl Salvatierra) as the alternate director from our sector, with the intention of having him fully share the responsibilities of office with the regular director. Raúl accompanies me at all of the board meetings, and he coordinates with me on the work of the Southern Water Team and the Social Committee in Defense of Life.

It seems to me very important and necessary to maintain social participation in the management of water, which happens, among other ways, through electing representatives of the population to the board of directors. These representatives have to be willing to remain accountable to the social organizations and the population in general. They have to be willing to permanently support the water committees and work with them to design institutional policies to apply within SEMAPA. I was clear about all this, and it seemed crucial to firmly establish this precedent in this first period so that it would persist in the future.

TL: What are the principal problems faced by SEMAPA? What does it lack? What does it need? And what attitude has the government taken toward SEMAPA?

LSG: The first challenge is to consolidate ourselves as what is legally termed a "Public Institution of Basic Services" without any profit motive, without interference or corruption from party politics, but with definite social participation in management. To ensure this, we have formalized all the hierarchical posts and, from the directors on down, a permanent monitoring of managerial positions has been established. Any practices constituting nepotism or clientism, for example, can be questioned. Furthermore, it is necessary to strengthen the participation of society in SEMAPA beyond the directors elected by the population. In this regard, a resolution presented by the *Coordinadora* that states that SEMAPA's directors should be elected by the Neighborhood Associations, which is still pending, ought to be approved. And it is necessary to encourage the work of the basic services representatives in the *Organizaciones Territoriales de Base* (OTBs; Local Territorial Organizations).

Another main challenge is to succeed in providing high-quality water service to all of the population twenty-four hours per day, to construct new sewer connections, and equitably distribute the costs. Currently, SEMAPA's system of drinking water reaches 62 percent of Cochabamba's citizenry, and only 58 percent are connected to the sewer system. And service in some zones of the city is pretty sporadic (twice a week, for two hours at a time).

In the first place we need to reduce the amount of water lost in the distribution system, which equals 55 percent of total production and results in unbilled water. Many users do not have meters, and there exists a significant number of clandestine connections to the water system. A physical loss of water also occurs in the oldest stretches of the system. Second, there exists an urgent need to expand the water and sewer network to include vast zones of the city, especially in southern Cochabamba. Simultaneously, we must increase the number of accessible water sources in order to be able to supply the whole population. We must also improve and increase the capacity of the water treatment system.

Finally, it is crucial to define the future relation between SEMAPA and the collective systems of water service—the neighborhood committees for drinking water—that exist in the zones to which SEMAPA does not presently extend. (In the south there are some forty water committees created and run by the communities themselves.) The current proposal is to maintain the existence of these communal committees, and to establish an alliance between them and SEMAPA, such that the municipal company provides them with water and they distribute it throughout their neighborhoods using their own networks. In this way, there would develop a real relationship of co-management between SEMAPA and the communal systems, in which specifically assigned responsibilities would exist for the technical and social aspects of drinking water management.

TL: What role has international support played during these years?

LSG: It has been extremely important and decisive for the planning and implementation of social participation policies as well as for the improvement of services—not only for SEMAPA but also for the neighborhood water committees. In November 2002, we held an International Seminar in Support of SEMAPA that included the participation of international groups from Canada, the United States, Brazil, and other countries, which marked the starting point of an international relationship that has proven key for SEMAPA.

Specifically, our collaboration has resulted in the co-management design structure mentioned above and in the strengthening of the water committees in the southern zone. Our international contacts have grown in recent years, and this has made it possible for us to receive economic assistance from solidarity groups in the US, Canada, and Spain. Their support has served to help us strengthen the water committees and to develop a strategy for integrating technical management and social management in the administration of drinking water.

Moreover, international support—which was so visible following the social victory represented by the Water War—has contributed to our ability to put pressure on the Bolivian government, the Department of Water and Sanitation, the diverse ministries overseeing aspects of water provision, and the mayor's office. It has also enabled pressure to be focused internally—within SEMAPA—to help us remain strong in our defense of the principles won in April 2000.

The legal battle of the anti-neoliberal social forces against Bechtel and the arbitration of the World Bank's ICRID (International Center for the Regulation of Investment Disputes) have also been strengthened because of international support. And the Cochabamba people themselves have felt supported in their struggle and internationally recognized for the principles and values they fought for and now wish to make permanent.

TL: How do you think people regard SEMAPA today?

LSG: People receive little information about what SEMAPA is doing, and they do not perceive a substantial improvement in their water and sewer service. Nevertheless, and despite the shortcomings we need to fix, there exists explicit public confidence in SEMAPA because it was saved from privatization by the sacrifice and struggle of the whole population, and because it is administered today with an important degree of social participation. A general attitude of patience persists. But, except in the southern zone, there is not a social consciousness that people should stay informed and participate in decision-making. They let SEMAPA

¡COCHABAMBA!

go about its work without clearly feeling that the collectivity has any co-responsibility for it. Only the most disadvantaged social groups have acquired a strong consciousness of their right and responsibility to participate in the decisions that affect basic services—and of the enormous risk that is run when people do not.

TL: What attitude have the financial institutions and the State adopted toward SEMAPA after the Water War?

LSG: Our victory in the Water War announced the defeat of the neoliberal principles which the international financial organizations support and advocate. And to the extent that the new self-managed SEMAPA is succeeding in realizing our goals, that defeat is becoming consolidated and visible. Statements such as "After the Water War, nothing is the same," made by representatives of the organizations themselves, testify to this. And our approval of credits from the International Development Bank demonstrates it as well. There we were able to negotiate conditions such as provisions for social participation—something that would not have even been considered before.

Nevertheless, these same institutions continue, through other means, to try to impose their conditions and torpedo the Cochabamban experience. They sometimes attempt to introduce private investment through cover entities that hide the real intention to privatize. For example, we receive constant offers of huge loans, and even donations, should we agree to accept entities in our operation that are closer to privatized businesses, such as the mixed (public/private) corporations. Or people initiate processes, without social participation, that would create joint ownership associations and would superimpose themselves on and derail more local and self-managing setups.

With similar intentions, the World Bank is "arbitrating" the dispute between *Aguas del Tunari* and the Bolivian State over the profits that were lost when Bechtel was thrown out of Cochabamba. (Bechtel is demanding $25 million in indemnities.) Or, in the same vein, institutions such as the Bolivian Internal Revenue Service, GRACO, and the City of Cochabamba have demanded the payment of back debts. Some of these debts were scheduled to be forgiven under the privatization contract with *Aguas del Tunari*. But now they are demanding repayment and, if we are forced to pay, it would immediately bankrupt SEMAPA.[1]

LUIS SÁNCHEZ-GÓMEZ

TL: To what extent is it legitimate to claim that the Water War has meant a setback in finding a solution for supplying water to Cochabamba's population?

LSG: That claim is absolutely false. *Aguas del Tunari* never showed any sign of willingness to invest in improving and expanding Cochabamba's basic services. For them, water and sewer "service" was just a business. They analyzed the supplying of water from the point of view of profitability. They didn't see things, therefore, as a problem of insufficient services, but rather as an opportunity for a lucrative business.

Aguas del Tunari's first step was to squeeze the maximum profit out of current clients by raising rates in an abusive and irrational way. With part of this income, they began investing in expanding the network at a pace dictated by business concerns. They did not intend to extend the network on the basis of social urgency and necessity, but rather on the basis of profitability. And given the condition of SEMAPA when they acquired it, and given the poverty of the majority of the population, *Aguas del Tunari* would have required years to expand the supply of water to the whole city. What's more, it became obvious that the great majority of the citizens would not be able to afford the services that *Aguas del Tunari* pretended to offer.

Contrary to what your question suggests, SEMAPA today is in fact expanding both drinking water and sewer services. We anticipate, on the basis of solid projections, adding twelve thousand new user accounts (approximately sixty thousand people) to our drinking water service in 2004. This will be possible because we have increased our water availability through developing new sources (an additional 200 liters per second). And during 2005 our available water will increase by another 500 l/s throughout the city—100 l/s from reducing losses in the feeder canals and 400 l/s from new surface sources—wells—and the improvement of existing ones.

In other words, five years after the Water War, we will have covered an extra 15 percent of the population (for a total of 75 percent of the city), and we will have increased the available supply of water by 70 percent. No one in Cochabamba believes that *Aguas del Tunari* could have done any better—even if they had wanted to.

¡COCHABAMBA!

TL: Oscar Olivera always speaks about the four principles that should guide SEMAPA: efficiency in its delivery of services; transparency in its operations; social participation in decision-making; and accessibility for everyone. How would you evaluate the implementation of these principles now that we are more than three years beyond the Water War?

LSG: Honestly, I believe that these four principles, which are indeed fundamental, do not make for the visible kind of advances and results which, again in all honesty, I believe have taken place. That is, the efficiency of SEMAPA is now much greater. The new legal structure and the greater social participation brought about by the *Coordinadora,* the formalizing of positions and responsibilities, the abilities of the managers and technicians, and the access to some economic resources through the credits necessary for investment have, I believe, all increased efficiency. But for the results of these new conditions to be measurable in concrete terms, we will need a longer time frame. Nevertheless, one unquestionable fact that demonstrates signs of efficiency is that service and product quality have improved over the past three years without any rate hikes.

SEMAPA's transparency is well-known, and, although more people can and should be involved, social participation in the running of SEMAPA has played a highly positive role in defining institutional policies. I refer here not only to the participation of Cochabambinos, but also to the technical cooperation from the international groups I mentioned. One example of this was the successful opposition by all the elected directors, who represent the population, to the proposal made by the commercial management to index our water rates to the dollar. Another example—one which concerns the question of social equity, access, and the needs of the less privileged sectors of the population—is the draft proposal for a new rate schedule. This draft will be submitted for study, correction, and approval to the social organizations prior to its implementation. And then there are the various projects of expanding the network in the city's southern zone. These have resulted from proposals made by locals and their neighborhood organizations, and they will involve the neighborhood water committees in the management and administration of the zone's drinking water.

LUIS SÁNCHEZ-GÓMEZ

TL: What is the biggest challenge that SEMAPA will face over the next two or three years, and what is your general assessment of the future of SEMAPA as a self-managed company?

LSG: The two biggest challenges, which are indissolubly linked to one another, are efficiency and social participation in the management. We cannot achieve one without simultaneously achieving the other—precisely because we need to achieve both in order to fulfill the best possible model of managing a basic service. In the coming years we will find out if the direction we have chosen is correct or not.

Before three years had passed, SEMAPA needed to incorporate new models of social participation into running the company. This is being accomplished in the south of the city through the involvement of those responsible for basic sanitation from each of the neighborhood organizations in SEMAPA. These accomplishments surely have succeeded in creating a wider and more efficient company.

If we follow the proposals of the international and national financial institutions, we will not have significantly increased our water production three years from now. However, if we do succeed in accessing a greater quantity of water, it is because we have followed other types of proposals coming from society as a whole. If we succeed in this goal without having turned to the condition-laden loans of the financial organizations, then we will have demonstrated once again that self-management is more efficient than the precarious dependency proposed by the theorists of privatization.

Luis Sánchez-Gómez serves on the board of directors of *Servicios Municipales de Agua Potable y Alcantarillado* (SEMAPA; Municipal Drinking Water and Sewer Services), Cochabamba's municipal water company. He is also a Jesuit father and the head parish priest of the Santa Vera Cruz neighborhood in Cochabamba. This interview was conducted by Tom Lewis in July 2003.

ENDNOTES

1. Recently the Internal Revenue Service has demanded payment of forty-five million bolivianos from SEMAPA.

SEMAPA
GLOBALIZING SOLIDARITY

A Report from the International Network

In April 2000, after the protests that are now known as the Water War, the Bolivian government announced the dissolution of their contract with *Aguas del Tunari* for control of Cochabamba's water system. During the following two-and-one-half years, *Servicios Municipales de Agua Potable y Alcantarillado* (SEMAPA; Municipal Drinking Water and Sewer Services) the municipal water company, focused on integrating the participation of the community into the management of the water system. The first phase of this process culminated in April 2002 with a new service contract between the government and SEMAPA. A new board, including three members chosen directly by the population, was created and a new manager was hired.[1]

These changes, which more directly involve the community in the direction of SEMAPA, form part of the overall perspective for the water company. After recovering the water company from a transnational corporation, the social movements of Cochabamba, assisted by international organizations, have worked to develop a model of municipal water service that can be a successful example of an alternative to privatization.

As part of this process, a network has been developed with union leaders, environmentalists, and social and neighborhood organizations. Ties with international institutions have also been developed. Stemming from encounters with Oscar Olivera during international events, such organizations realized the need to support SEMAPA's development, especially its technical and managerial aspects.

One step was to organize an international seminar to analyze SEMAPA and design strategies that would improve social participation. The objective of the seminar, which took place in 2003, was to provide a forum for SEMAPA, popular organizations, social leaders, and international representatives of organizations to search for and develop a shared and efficient administration of the water system.

During two meetings in the installations of SEMAPA and a third in the offices of the Coalition in Defense of Water and Life, SEMAPA diagnosed their different areas of work. The social representatives presented what they perceived as the difficulties faced in providing water and sewage service, and representatives of international organizations, such as CORSAN (a Brazilian water company), shared their inspirational experiences in fighting against privatization.

SEMAPA'S OPERATION

After SEMAPA gave their presentation on the current state of the company and their service provision, the international observers highlighted what they felt to be the current strengths and weaknesses of SEMAPA. These observations were supplemented by local participants. Strengths include good coverage by the sewage system, which serves 50 percent of the population; a management structure which guarantees the participation of representatives elected by the community; and the presence of local technicians with excellent abilities and potential. SEMAPA was also observed to possess very good physical installations, equipment, and vehicles, which indicated a healthy financial capacity.

SEMAPA possesses a body of knowledge which enables it to properly analyze and expand the water system. A digitalized survey of the water distribution system, theoretical studies, and projects for the enlargement of the main storage system and distribution networks to provide for the southern zone are valuable resources which will help the company progress.

The proposals to the Inter-American Development Bank (IDB) for resources to acquire nearly seventeen thousand water meters, as well as to more generally strengthen programs and extend the water distribution and sewage system, were also positive developments.

SEMAPA has worked to ensure its leadership has a high level of popular participation. The newly hired general manager has offered to increase popular participation by formulating a work plan to expand the drinkable water and sewage system. In general, there is an agreement on the need to reevaluate all aspects of the present systems and on the urgency of developing environmental education and social communication.

An area of major discussion and concern was the rate structure. It currently does not correspond to a rational maximization of income, recuperation of costs, or a social evaluation of the market. As a consequence, there exists great resentment among the public regarding the present rate structure and SEMAPA's inability to explain (and to justify) it. International literature and experience suggest the urgency of a revision.

While SEMAPA is currently researching the possibilities of modifying the present rate structure, it is not clear that an internal capacity for this revision exists. The rate structure should be reevaluated under guidelines pertaining to social justice, economic equilibrium, and rational use of the water. The relation between consumption and rates remains important and needs to be taken into account; those who consume more should pay more.

General operations of SEMAPA need to be tightened. Procedures should be adopted that allow for institution of a twenty-four-hour water monitoring system and accurate measurement of water produced and distributed. Along with increased monitoring, steps should be taken to control losses. Strategies and routine procedures should be developed to investigate leaks, check for theft, and document water lines to new customers. An analysis of the interrelationship of distribution sectors with pumping stations and collection sites is also needed.

As increasing the social control of SEMAPA by the community is one of the goals of the reorganization, mechanisms of dialogue should be improved between SEMAPA and the community. A forum for the exchange of ideas and information needs to be developed. Similarly, the specific absence of workshops that allow workers to participate in the management process should be addressed. Mechanisms that guarantee the education and the involvement of workers should be developed.

There is an urgent need to improve the flow of information and the relations among the diverse areas of SEMAPA (projects, operations, commercial, administrative, and financial). Strategies for integration and joint development in strategic planning and follow-through should be adopted.

Observers also commented on relations between SEMAPA and the mayor's office and recommended a strategy to improve them. This strategy should be urgently adopted so SEMAPA and the mayor's office can work together to solve broader environmental problems in addition to issues concerning the water and sewage system. SEMAPA is not yet involved with local businesspeople; new and better mechanisms should be sought to achieve their participation.

A series of observations on SEMAPA's relations with the community and, in particular, with the independent water networks in the south, were offered along with recommendations to address weak points. It is important for SEMAPA to support the independent systems and be dedicated to the technical analysis of these systems. Considering both the long- and short-term municipal-wide vision regarding the incorporation of the independent systems into SEMAPA's main system, it is important that the technically deficient support system be strengthened. SEMAPA's support of these systems, as well as the technical knowledge that will be gained in the process, will insure credibility for future negotiations. Discussion with community leaders should address the possibility of carrying out joint projects

The situation of the southern zone of the city was considered critical and so it was recommended to immediately improve services in that sector in a way compatible with the long-term project. Some emergency measures already in development include hydrological studies, utilization of deep wells, assisting the region's main distributors and networks of distribution, constructing common tanks, and the capitalization of the resources advanced by users for new connections.

This issue of increasing the water supply or extending the sewage system should be closely analyzed in terms of short- and long-term investments and with community involvement. The community reacted strongly when they heard that a large amount of financial resources would be used to extend the sewage system while a big part of the city itself does not have treated water.

It also would be beneficial for SEMAPA to discuss with society, the mayor, and internally the possibilities of self-financing in order to reduce the dependence on foreign investors, to optimize costs, and to enable a greater autonomy of the public utility.

A further area where it was recommended that SEMAPA increase its focus and resources was on environmental issues. The role of a public business is to discuss and disseminate environmental education concepts within society. Participants said that SEMAPA should be more involved in environmental issues through the development of specific programs or by directly providing environmental education in the schools, associations, and the general community.

It is evident that managing the water as an independent system, without consideration of the ecosystem, is not appropriate in this day and age. In such a context, we are required to reconsider the form in which hydrological studies are carried out, including an evaluation of the collection capacity of water sources. Various studies have been carried out by academic groups which could give information on this topic. To date, however, no effort has been made to gather this information or to integrate it into a global diagnosis.

There is a general recognition of the importance of maintaining and rehabilitating ecosystems. Several people mentioned with approval the partial reforestation programs SEMAPA has supported. They also lamented the numerous forest fires, which apparently occurred as a result of local conflicts over the use of the soil and ownership of the land, and which have resulted in big setbacks.

There is no systematic planning of the use of spring and underground water. Although one needs permission for the exploitation of wells, effective supervision apparently does not take place. Adequate knowledge of these resources is lacking, and there exists no understanding of the long-term dynamics of renewal. There is also no appropriate needs assessment for the regional ecosystem.

The absence of legislation relative to the divisions and occupations of areas was noted, as well as the need for endowment of urban infrastructure (water, sewage, rain drainage, and so on) in these areas. Among other problems, there is no effective regional-use plan. Some people mentioned that it falls to each local administration to renegotiate the "protected elevation" in the hills and mountains surrounding the metropolitan area, thus causing a progressive invasion of fragile zones by new residents.

It is fundamental to consider the necessity of redesigning the present systems for the reuse and recycling of water and, above all, to take into account a more rational use of water, including the use of gray water, filters, and the collection of rainwater. Studies should examine the rationality of installing adequately designed parallel circuits and include community practices and the issues mentioned above as part of a new design for the local hydraulic system.

RESULTS, CONCLUSIONS, AND RECOMMENDATIONS

The series of meetings concluded by offering specific recommendations in four areas to address SEMAPA's most pressing needs. The recommendations focused on improving communications, between SEMAPA and the community and within SEMAPA, on establishing an environmental education campaign, and on meeting current water needs.

A survey of the population was recommended in order to obtain a qualitative analysis of popular perceptions of the present operations of SEMAPA, to prioritize areas for improvement (water or sewage), and, in particular, to determine what payment conditions exist for financing. Furthermore, SEMAPA should develop a strategy to distribute and improve the accessibility of its technical, financial, administrative, and planning information. Simultaneously, as a symbol of commitment to these concepts, SEMAPA should incorporate principles of control and social participation into its official mission.

To deepen communication and cooperation between the community and SEMAPA, a series of forums for dialogue among SEMAPA's managers, social leaders, committees on water, and the citizenry in general should be established. These forums would facilitate the exchange of ideas and knowledge and generalize the challenges faced by SEMAPA and the community. Similar public spaces should be created to discuss questions of self-financing, social water rates, and SEMAPA's budget, among other issues.

There also should be discussion forums with the goal of enriching the internal dialogue within SEMAPA. Management and workers should meet to strengthen cooperation, to ensure the voice of labor is heard in business decisions, and for both sides to renew their commitment to achieve the mission of the business.

¡COCHABAMBA!

A department of education could be created inside SEMAPA to head up an environmental education campaign for the population of Cochabamba. This campaign, which would include the management and workers of SEMAPA, might produce and disseminate educational materials and organize seminars. Furthermore, to ensure SEMAPA develops in environmentally sustainable ways, a team of SEMAPA technicians, investigators (university students, for example), and experts in environmental health would work with communities to circulate environmental knowledge and to undertake analyses of SEMAPA's strengths and weaknesses.

And, as part of its core mission, SEMAPA should work to alleviate current water shortages. Support for existing self-generated projects will form an important part of these efforts. To guarantee the successful integration of these systems into SEMAPA's future water network, an exchange of skills is needed now in which SEMAPA contributes its technical knowledge to help communities with the management of their own water systems. The communities would contribute experiences with their social models and participatory management to enable these practices to be incorporated within the management of SEMAPA. This exchange and support would serve to create a cooperative and constructive relationship between SEMAPA and the community.

The investigation into the interim steps that could provide water to communities with no service, particularly in the south of the town, should proceed. In order for these efforts to succeed, these steps would have to be implemented under a participatory model similar to that already being utilized in communities with their own systems.

International support for SEMAPA should continue to be cultivated and viewed as a resource. CORSAN, in particular, can offer support to SEMAPA because of the knowledge and experience it has acquired over the years and through the numerous problems it has overcome. The possibility of creating an "Inter-American team" for Cochabamba has also been proposed as a way of solidifying international support.

At the end of the conference, a work team comprising various neighborhood groups, the planning manager, members of the board, and members of the *Coordinadora* was created to follow-up on these results.

In December 2002, the *Coordinadora* and SEMAPA organized a seminar which, for the first time since April 2000, brought together neighbors, water activists, and SEMAPA managers and workers. This group joined with supporters from Brazil, Mexico, and Canada in order to evaluate SEMAPA's performance.[2] The event was called, "International Seminar in Support of SEMAPA: Globalizing Solidarity." A version of this document was presented at the closing session of the seminar.

ENDNOTES

1. The local water board is made up of two representatives from the mayor's office including the mayor, a representative from the worker's union, a representative from the College of Professionals, and three members of the community elected from the three municipal districts.

2. The coordinating team for the seminar included Luis Sánchez Gómez, Raúl Salvatierra, and Ricardo Villazón, from the board of SEMAPA; Oscar Olivera from the *Coordinadora* and the *Fabriles*; Ing. Rafael Valdez, Manager of Planning, and Norma Barrera representing SEMAPA; and Marcela Olivera from the *Coordinadora* and the Fourth Interval Center. In addition to the coordinating team the following institutions and organizations participated: Three representatives of *Companhia Riograndense of Water and Basic Services* (CORSAN, Water and Sanitation Company of Rio Grande do Sul) from Brazil; Municipal Services Project of Canada and Holland (who supported the organization of the seminar, but could not attend); one representative of the Metropolitan Autonomous University (Mexico); one representative of the Polaris Institute (Canada); the General Manager, six Area Managers, twenty worker representatives, and the members of SEMAPA's Board of Directors (Cochabamba); members from ten neighborhood water committees based in southeast Cochabamba; fourteen representatives from the Vigilance Committee of the Cercado; and seventeen neighborhood leaders.

¡OUR REALITY AND OUR DREAMS!

THE NEW WORLD
OF LABOR

The academic fantasies of some intellectuals and the political wish-fulfillments of some party leaders would have it that blue- and white-collar workers no longer exist in Bolivia. In this "fantasy" we have all been magically transformed into merchants and our country is one grand and happy marketplace. Despite such liberal prejudices about the de-proletarianization of society, the Bolivian working class, far from shrinking, has grown enormously in size. While the number of factory workers in light industry, for example, initially declined as a result of DS 21060 and the onset of neoliberal economic policies, workers in that sector produce approximately 17 percent of the Gross Domestic Product (GDP).[1]

THE WORKING CLASS BY THE NUMBERS

The facts are both stubborn and overwhelming. There exist more than 354,000 wage workers in light industry across the country, contracted directly by small, medium, and large manufacturing companies, and about that same number, or even more, work in subcontracted light industry jobs or in sweatshops. If we add to these workers the number of full-time, subcontracted, and clandestine workers in other branches of the economy (mining, energy, construction, services), then, in 1997, we are talking about 3.5 million workers in a country of eight million people.[2] This is the approximate number of workers affected by changes in labor laws.

If it is true that a reduction occurred in the number of workers organized in unions and concentrated in large workplaces, it is also true that over the 1990s an inverse process of "re-proletarianization" unfolded within the economic and social structures of the country. In numerical terms, the total number of workers in the manufacturing industries of the capital cities climbed from 83,000 in 1986 to 150,000 in 1991, to 231,000 in 1995, and to 390,000 in 1997.[3] According to the National Bureau of Industry, in 2001 approximately 33 percent of workers were concentrated in factories with more than thirty employees, while another 49 percent could be found in workshops with between one and four employees.[4]

In terms of its contribution to GDP, mining production—which has suffered the worst effects of the neoliberal reforms, with falling mineral prices and numerous pit closures—has jumped from 3.7 percent of GDP in 1986 to 5.6 percent in 1996.[5] Workers in the mining sector went from 47,000 in 1986 to 74,000 in 1991, and the majority of the remaining workers are found in cooperative, as opposed to state-owned, mines.[6] Petroleum and natural gas have also risen as percentages of GDP.[7] Transportation and communications have moved from 8.3 percent of GDP in 1985 to 10 percent in 1997.[8]

Productive sectors such as industry, transportation, telecommunication, construction, and, to a certain extent, small and medium-sized private mining operations all possess an economic relevance today that is greater than ten or twenty years ago. Similarly, the number of wage workers who sell their labor power is much higher than it was ten years ago. And yet popular perception would have us believe just the opposite: that there are no wage laborers, there is no wage labor, and industrial production is irrelevant.

THE EROSION OF CLASS IDENTITY AND SOLIDARITY

How can we explain this kind of historical delirium, one that affects not only a certain gang of intellectuals but also experienced trade unionists?

Almost invisibly, Bolivia has been converted into a semi-industrial workshop in which workers themselves do not realize their social power and economic importance. Neoliberal reforms have *changed* the world of work, but they have not *shrunk* it. Neoliberalism has, rather, fragmented and transformed the conditions of labor. Beginning with the structural reforms of 1985, we have seen a general restructuring of the relations between civil society and the state and, in particular, of labor relations within the industrial plants. We are speaking here not only of privatization, of the change in the property form of such enterprises, but also, and above all, of the modification of management relations in the forms of hiring, in the flexible use of the workforce, in production techniques, and even in the mode of labor organization itself.

At this juncture there is no doubt that we are witnessing the emergence of a new urban working class. This "new" working class is characterized by the changed habits of production that are necessary to keep a job or cover contract requirements. Such changes include the loss of older established rights, such as job security and the eight-hour day. The growing fragmentation of conditions in which production activities take place, and the uncertainty and insecurity of employment, makes each member a "traveling" worker, bouncing among the small factory, commercial workplace, agricultural labor, and back to the shop floor. The growing predominance of young workers in the workplace willing to accept the bosses' current requirements is another result. And, finally, the basis for formation of class identity has changed as a result of these experiences of dispersion, atomization, and insecurity. In short, we are entitled to speak of a new working class because, materially and organizationally, it is different from the urban working class that began to develop in the years preceding the revolution of 1952 and continued through 1985.

It is on the basis of these profound transformations that we have witnessed an erosion and weakening of traditional union structures, as well as an increase in competition and division among workers. These changes have given rise to the impossibility of shaping a sense of class identity and practicing solidarity in the struggles over demands. The statistics are conclusive. They reveal, in terms of its percentage of the population as a whole, both an absolute and relative increase of the labor sector over the past nineteen years.[9] Yet, the social weight and significance of this population has diminished tremendously. The new working class has, so far, found it extremely difficult to project itself as an active social subject with sufficient personality to launch convincing mobilizations, to generate demands that motivate large numbers, or, with even less success, to put forward practical proposals that incorporate the demands of other social sectors.

This situation developed because the working class as a whole has been restructured in terms of its organization, consciousness, and culture by business interests that seek to make it submissive and powerless. They have succeeded to the extent that the working class itself cannot seem to find the path out of its disorganization and fear of the bosses. For these reasons, it has become indispensable to understand the new structure of labor. Only by understanding the new methods of workplace management that keep workers separated, the new modes of hiring that undermine and destroy hard-won benefits, the quantity of workers in each enterprise, and the technological changes that have changed the workplace by increasing labor and productivity can we have a clear overview of how the new exploitation functions and how the new dominion of capital imposes itself on workers.

With such a radiograph of the workplace conditions confronting today's working class, we can successfully discover the dynamics of each branch of industry as well as the needs and demands of different sectors of workers. Such a study will also provide convincing data on the loss of rights and the illegal implications of flexibilized labor. We will have the information to argue our position when the bosses attempt to change labor laws. And we will be able to involve the public in discussions about the bosses' abuse of workers and win their social support to restrict the bosses' power. The campaign to collect facts and information will also help workers, in the interest of achieving common objectives, become more conscious of the problems suffered by their fellow workers, with whom it remains urgent and indispensable to create links of solidarity and support.

A radiograph of the new structure of business and the position of the working class within it will show how far the bosses have advanced in their imprisonment of workers. It will also reveal the limits and contradictions of the bosses' abuses, thus facilitating their unmasking and repudiation by workers organized in communities of struggle.

STRENGTHENING CONSCIOUSNESS AND MORALE

With these benefits in mind, the *Fabriles* has undertaken work in three important areas that acknowledge our own possibilities and limitations. We have worked to systematize the information we gather; to carry out informational campaigns denouncing and making visible the current problematic of labor; and to strengthen rank and file organizations.

We have visited local unionized and non-unionized factories and workshops. In the latter cases, it was the workers themselves who requested that we come to see their workplace conditions. We have documented the inhuman exploitation of scores of workers, particularly women and minors. We have recorded the enormous numbers of temporary workers with no rights or benefits. And we have witnessed the competition between permanent workers and the temporaries, the extended work schedules, the payment of in-kind wages, and the other wrongs that male and female workers endure today.

In addition to our efforts, we have been able to count on the participation of various media workers, who have worked to reflect the living and working conditions we have discovered. Their words and images have been widely circulated, and, since their employers wield substantial power, not without risk.

The task we have set ourselves now is the strengthening of workers' morale and organization. We are returning to the non-unionized factories with the goal of evaluating our earlier visits. In some workplaces, for example, we have confirmed new layoffs; in others we have seen an improvement in working conditions; and in some we have even found that the bosses apologized for the insecure working conditions and promised to improve the situation.

Building identity and solidarity among the new working class requires special efforts to unite older workers with younger workers and with the most vulnerable sectors of the working population. The "flexibilization of labor," which is a term that means nothing other than the elimination of workers' rights, hurts all workers, but women workers and child laborers suffer the most.

Young workers fit the bosses' new requirements of efficiency and submission. Efficiency and obedience are apparently more desired than experience and wisdom. Young workers are also "polyvalent" workers; that is they have no fixed job or trade. They may well have an undergraduate degree. These are the new characteristics of Bolivian workers in general.

Besides their youth, women workers, who now compose 20 percent of the manufacturing sector, have an additional common denominator.[10] Whether a single mom, a widow, or an abandoned wife, in Bolivian society each woman worker bears a great family responsibility, with children, parents, or siblings depending on her earnings. This increases the risk and penalties of her resistance.

This makes female labor the most sought after by the bosses, and, simply by being female, women workers earn approximately 40 percent less than a man working the same job.[11] Additionally, pregnancy is prohibited. If a woman worker does become pregnant, she is not allowed pre- or post-natal time off; indeed, she must work until the very last days of her pregnancy. Women workers—pregnant or not—receive no type of on-the-job protection against insecticides and other chemical products in the flower industry, glue in the shoe factories, acrylics in the textile manufacturers, heavy lifting in the ceramic plants, dyes in the clothing industry, or humidity in the chicken processing plants. Sexual harassment, moreover, permeates every workplace. Because of these harsh realities, women workers are the most vulnerable and suffer the most violations of their basic human and labor rights.

The older wage worker with a permanent contract, concentrated in the large enterprises, unionized with guaranteed labor rights, and with recognition from the state, is rapidly ceasing to exist. Simultaneously, we are witnessing the growth of a new type of wage worker, more widespread and economically important than before. Presently, this type of worker lacks organization, is spatially fragmented, fearful, without legitimate representation before the state (except for his or her vote as a citizen), and unrecognized in terms of his or her economic value to society.

THE IDEOLOGY AND REALITY OF LABOR FLEXIBILIZATION

One front of the attack against Bolivian working people is the aggressive campaign which claims that current labor-friendly laws are hurting Bolivia's growth. This attack, which seeks to modify labor relations in our country, has been unleashed by reactionary sectors of Bolivian business and the government, who employ several arguments. The bosses and politicians criticize the large number of regulations and safeguards that currently exist in the labor field, claiming they make interpretation and application difficult. They go on to assert that unequal treatment of worker and owner exists—that existing law is too protective of the worker, leading to permanent employment. They point to the appearance of new types of jobs resulting from changes in the way production is organized as a reason for pursuing flexibilization, and they question the lack of correspondence between current labor legislation and the new, reduced role assigned to the state under privatization. Finally, the bosses and politicians consider inadequate the treatment given by existing law to social benefits, contracts, rights, and responsibilities. For them, these provisions simply increase labor costs.

All of these arguments are aimed, their proponents say, at ensuring significant increases in productivity and at establishing a clear relation between productivity and earnings. At rock bottom, they call into question what they call the workers' accumulation of benefits, which is viewed as having a negative impact on investment.

The validity of such arguments, however, has turned out to be false. Since the implementation of the neoliberal model in 1985, the industrial sector has grown significantly, with production accounting for 33 percent of GDP in 2003.[12]

The quality of jobs, however, is no better than before. Workers now perform more work for lower wages. The average number of hours worked per week has risen from forty-four in 1987 to fifty-two by the early 1990s, and the gross volume of production increased by 300 percent.[13] We are forced to navigate our way through a sea of insecurity, temporary jobs, and subcontracted labor. In 1996 real wages, indexed to 1987 prices, were valued at one half their 1984 value.[14] The minimum wage decreased in value by 40 percent in eighteen years.[15] The quality of life for working-class families has deteriorated. Now wives and children must work merely to cover the basic necessities. This fact has made the education and training of young people extremely difficult. The gap between rich and poor has widened notoriously.

All of this renders the bosses' arguments exceedingly strange. They say things like, "Job security and social benefits signify elevated costs that dampen investment," and "Lower investment impedes the creation of more and better jobs." They go on to insist, "It's good for everyone to allow flexible modes of hiring and to decrease benefits because this stimulates investment, and that way there are more and higher quality jobs because we make greater profits."

We workers can do no less than ask ourselves "Is this true?" And we have to ask the bosses, "Do you mean that social benefits and job security block the creation of more and better jobs? Then how is it possible that, when these rights are taken from us, we still don't see any new jobs?"

The bosses argue that by reducing labor costs (benefits, overtime, night shifts, Sundays off, vacations) they can increase workers' pay. But we workers ask, "How is that possible?" It is clear that, if the bosses reduce labor costs, productivity goes up, not because there is increased investment, or because production is organized in a more rational manner, or even because transportation outlets are improved or the bureaucratic costs of permits and bookkeeping go down. Productivity rises for one simple reason: more work is being forced out of each worker for less pay. How could it be possible in these conditions to achieve increases in workers' pay, when the increase of the capitalists' profits depends precisely on the opposite?

Neoliberalism was not born with the drafting of DS 21060 by a cabinet filled with social-climbing technocrats. It was born when a faction of the local business class bet that the maintenance and advance of its interests was assured by its association with and subordination to branches of foreign capital. It was born when the bosses proved themselves willing to raffle off more than sixty years of social capital accumulated by the efforts of the Bolivian people.[16]

The bosses not only have fundamental economic interests; they also have clear political interests. It is no accident that what characterizes the new epoch of neoliberalism is the systematic assault on and destruction of the labor movement as part of an attempt to dampen struggle and resistance. Military defeat in Calamarca, mine closures, a furious campaign of forced retirements to get rid of the workers with the most organizing experience, and the implementation of free labor contracting are all testimonies to a vicious bosses' offensive against workers' rights.[17]

These political changes, in turn, bring about a set of economic changes that only reinforce the former. After privatization, the so-called "relocation" threw out on the streets twenty thousand of the twenty-seven thousand workers in the state-owned mines. The privatized mining industry subsequently reduced its workforce by half. Oil and refinery workers, construction workers, and railway workers—those who form the iron core of the Bolivian labor movement—are still swelling the ranks of the unemployed. The percentage of workers with a permenant job has dropped from 71 percent in 1989 to 29 percent in 1996.[18] The free contracting of labor decreed in 1985 has created an atmosphere of complete uncertainty and total insecurity among workers. Free hiring and firing has not improved employment but has rendered it more uncertain and insecure.

No one—not the government, not the bosses, not society as a whole—can fail to recognize that the flexible use of labor has been imposed on Bolivian workers. Job security has been replaced by subcontracted labor and temporary hires, which do not provide for retirement, social security, health insurance, severance pay, or other benefits. The eight-hour day is not respected. Women as well as men are required to work nine to twelve hours per day, including weekends and holidays. And wages no longer include overtime, holiday pay, Sunday bonuses, shift differentials, family benefits, or seniority and experience. Such so-called labor costs, which, in practice, are none other than the rights we have had taken away, account for less than 10 percent of the total cost of production, including technical and administrative salaries.[19] Thus the bosses' arguments for the necessity of flexibilization are a sham.

Yet there exists another concrete reality: the labor of this great mass of men and women workers—young and old, each with insecure futures—is responsible for generating the recent growth in the industrial sector. It is their labor that has made the economy grow. Nevertheless, obvious questions remain: Has any of this growth improved the lives of the working population? Does the worker and his or her family have access to, and derive enjoyment from, more resources than before? Are the well-being and education of young workers higher priorities than before?

WHAT CAN WE DO?

As we have seen, one tactic the government has used to attack workers is to change labor laws. What can we do as workers in the face of such attempts to change labor laws and further strip us of our rights? There exist three possibilities: defend the General Law on Labor as it is; negotiate aspects and details of the version of the law put forward by the bosses and the government; or elaborate and fight for our own New General Law on Labor.

We believe that the last option is the best one. To defend the existing law without any changes is a dead end. To negotiate aspects or details of the law as proposed by the bosses and the government would signify our acceptance of their plans and terms. Only a law elaborated, publicly disseminated, and actively fought for by workers will guarantee the preservation of the rights won by our fathers and grandfathers. Only the fight for a law drafted by workers themselves will broaden legislation to include presently unprotected workers. Only a law we create will defend workers' rights within the new flexibilized forms of production.

As we work to elaborate and fight for our own General Law on Labor it should contain three fundamental principles: protection of the worker; state intervention to ensure compliance with labor laws; and the inalienability of rights. Beyond these, we also consider that the law should embody the following features: guaranteed job security; the possibility of a just wage—one that will allow us to take care of our families and have access to health care, education, and housing; respect for the eight-hour day, so that we can rest eight hours and share the other eight hours with our families and community; respect for social benefits and the right to organize; and obligatory compliance with the General Law on Labor and collective bargaining.

The fight for such laws is important because they establish norms and procedures for different aspects of social, political, and economic life. Every law is written in a particular historical moment and reflects the relations of social forces of its time. Laws register the ability of different groups or classes to establish the "rules of the game" according to their interests. If one group or class is stronger than the others, it will be the one which determines what these rules are.

The rules of the game—or laws—are important. If a law favors the possibility of organizing a union, or having a secure job, it helps workers defend themselves and advance their cause. If the laws make it difficult for workers to organize or to defend themselves, it hurts their cause. Laws do not guarantee results, but they do have an important impact on the process of fighting for social justice. Hence, it is extremely important to ensure that laws reflect the interests of workers and, afterwards, to see that they are enforced.

Our proposal concerning what we want labor relations to be, as with all our organizing activity, should serve as a vehicle for raising workers' consciousness about their rights, for showing workers the contemporary reality of work, for organizing, and for mobilizing in order to defend our rights.

A version of this essay was originally presented by Oscar Olivera at the meeting hall of the *Fabriles* on December 10, 1998.

ENDNOTES

1. Table: Bolivia: Producto Interno Bruto por Año Según Actividad Económica, 1990-2003, Instituto Nacionales de Estadistica, La Paz. Accessed at http://www.ine.gov.bo (September 2004).
2. Gregorio Iriarte, *Análisis Crítico de la Realidad,* (Cochabamba: Kipus, 2004), 406; see also www.ine.gov.bo and www.cedla.org.
3. *Cámara Nacional de Industria: Reporte de 1990,* La Paz.
4. Table: Estructura de la Población Ocupada por Rama de Actividad y Sexo Segun Sector del Mercado de Trabajo 1992-2001, Instituto Nacionales de Estadistica, La Paz. Accessed at http://www.ine.gov.bo (September 2004).
5. Table: Producto Interno Bruto, Extracción de Minas y Canteras, Instituto Nacional de Estadística, La Paz, 2000.
6. Table: Fuerza de Trabajo Sector Minero. Boletin, Secretaria Nacional de Mineria, 1995, Instituto Nacionales de Estadistica, La Paz. Accessed at http://www.ine.gov.bo (September 2004).
7. Table: Producto Interno Bruto, Extraccion de Minas y Canteras, Instituto Nacional de Estadística, La Paz, 2000.
8. Table: Producto Interno Bruto por Actividad Económica, Instituto Nacional de Estadística, La Paz, 2000.
9. Iriate, *Análisis Crítico de la Realidad,* 408; see also Table: Encuesta Nacional de Empleo (Periodos 1986, 1996, 1997, 2002), Instituto Nacionales de Estadistica, La Paz. Accessed at http://www.ine.gov.bo (September 2004).
10. Iriate, *Análisis Crítico de la Realidad,* 511.
11. Iriate, *Análisis Crítico de la Realidad,* 511.
12. "Bolivia" *Enciclopedia Encarta,* s.v. "Bolivia," http://es.encarta.msn.com/text_761563800___13/Bolivia.html (September 2004).
13. *Evolucion de las Jornadas Laborales Semanales Promedio por Rama de Actividad 1992-2001* (Fuente: Encuesta Integrada de Hogares, INE, 1992).
14. Executive Summary, Bolivia: Employment and Social Protection Policies and Programmes, Organización Internacional del Trabajo,

http://www.oitandina.org.pe/about/success/infbolivia2.html
(September 2004).

15. Iriarte, *Análisis Crítico de la Realidad,* 376.
16. I am referring here to the privatizations of *Yacimientos Petrolíferos Fiscales Bolivianos* (YPFB), *Corporación Minera de Bolivia* (COMIBOL), *Corporación Boliviana de Fomento* (CBF), *Empresa Nacional de Telecomunicaciones* (ENTEL), *Empresa Nacional de Ferrocarriles, and others.*
17. In the year following DS 21060, when a policy of relocation began, Bolivian miners organized a march called "The March for Life." Thousands and thousands of miners converged in a march on La Paz. In one section, called Calamarca, of the road between Oruro and La Paz the army surrounded the miners and ordered them to go back. Many leaders of the march said they should reach an agreement with the army commanders. Others said that to do so would mean a crushing defeat for the Bolivian social movements. In the end, the miners retreated without a confrontation, even though they, too, were armed.

I believe that if the miners had succeeded in reaching La Paz, the history of our country would have been different. As in 1952, there would have been a kind of revolution. Instead, the miners' defeat signaled the beginning of a new epoch in Bolivia—the era of neoliberalism.
18. Iriarte, *Análisis Crítico de la Realidad,* 407, 560.
19. Carlos Arce, *Costos Laborales y Competitividad en la Industria Boliviana,* (La Paz: CEDLA, 1999).

A POLITICAL THESIS

In the early 1980s, capitalism in the countries of the North entered into acute economic crisis, with the profitability of capitalist enterprises steadily falling. Although the most powerful businesspeople in the world—the owners of the huge international consortiums—continued to invest capital and to increase production, their profits did not grow as they had before.

It was at this juncture that the neoliberal offensive began, and we are still suffering under it. Neoliberalism is simply an overall strategic plan of global capitalism to restore higher rates of profit on its investments and business operations. By global capitalism I mean the most powerful national governments and the international institutions that control the economy of the planet—the IMF, the World Bank, the transnational corporations, and so on.

NEOLIBERALISM

On a planetary scale, the bosses' neoliberal plan has been based on three principles: reorganizing the production process, reducing the cost of labor, and liberalizing the circulation of capital and commodities.

Reorganizing the production process has meant the "shrinking" of businesses: the drastic reduction of the number of unionized workers by means of wave after wave of layoffs; the hiring of new, non-unionized workers without labor rights; and the demand for greater productivity from those workers who keep their jobs. It has also meant the fragmentation of the production process into smaller and more "agile" firms, in which workers are not concentrated in large contingents and hence are forced to passively accept the working conditions imposed by the bosses.

Technological innovations, the creation of a new type of workforce exploited more for its mental and creative capacities than for its physical ability, the formation of work teams with relative autonomy to meet the bosses' quotas, and, in general, post-Fordism—the restructuring of labor in order to get rid of "downtimes"—are the principal material mechanisms that carry the capitalist plan forward.

In practice, reducing the cost of labor has entailed rolling back the acquired rights and gains of the labor movement. It has resulted in raising the retirement age, imposing salary caps, slashing workers' benefits, lengthening the work week, and demanding greater output per worker. Bolivian bosses and politicians have found numerous ways to cheapen the value of labor power. That is, they have succeeded in insuring that workers receive less for the same amount of work or even for a greater amount.

The globalization of the world for capitalism and the privatization of enterprises and natural resources is what is meant by the phrase "liberalizing the circulation of capital and commodities." During the last twenty years, the most powerful businesses have pressured nations to take down their old national borders and protections and permit investments and commodities to circulate "freely." In this way, multinational enterprises not only are able to invest their capital in places and countries where they can get the highest profits, but they are also able to get workers of one nation to compete with workers of other nations. A business can currently have its products made in a country where conditions for workers are abysmal and salaries low (such as in southeast Asia, China, or Latin America) and later take them and sell them in other places to ensure maximum profit.

Similarly, under the world trade agreements, the enterprises that produce the greatest number of commodities at the least cost can now export their products to the rest of the world without encountering any tariff restrictions. This damages not only the nation's small businesses but also the workers themselves, who either lose their jobs or have to put up with salary cuts so that the local enterprise can compete with the foreign ones. In reality, free trade is nothing but the dictatorship of the business class and the largest, most powerful governments over the smaller nations and their more fragile economies. This, broadly speaking, is globalization.

Moreover, globalization has shaped conditions in which enormous portions of the wealth of individual countries that used to be public property have become the private property of various transnationals. In short, wealth that used to form part of the public patrimony—the airlines, railroads, telecommunications system, the production and distribution of electricity, and, in some countries, the refining and even production of petroleum—have passed over into the hands of private businesses. Privatization, which can occur through various mechanisms such as the creation of joint ventures between the state and private capital, the sale of stock, and direct auction, all has the same result.

What has happened is a reduction on a global scale of the amount of resources to fund social programs, that is, the monies that are used to fund a certain level of public welfare. The gigantic profits produced by all of these undertakings which, in past decades, constituted the pillar supporting state expenditures on public services, the development of urban infrastructure, and the like, are now monopolized by transnational corporations. The transnationals now reinvest these profits in new businesses or privatize others, thus consolidating the processes of private accumulation and concentration of wealth to an incredible degree: the richest 1 percent of the world's population earns as much as the poorest 57 percent.[1]

It is clear that neoliberalism, or neoliberal globalization, is an economic, technological, organizational, political, and cultural strategy of the business world. Its aim is to find new ways of disciplining the productive power of the worker, which had begun to weaken the employers' old methods of exploitation and profit making. The bosses intend to overcome their reduced rate of profit by making workers bear the cost through lower standards of living, reduced salaries, flexibilized work schedules, and anything else they can do to destroy workers' rights. This is why neoliberalism will never mean economic development or social well-being for workers—its basis is the intensified exploitation of workers.

The neoliberal reforms that have been imposed across the planet constitute a bosses' offensive so ferocious and so far-reaching that the working class of virtually every country was—at least initially, and is still for the most part—paralyzed by the combined attack of business and government. In the last few years, however, workers and the other dominated sectors of society have begun to find ways to resist, to fight, and to regain self-respect in the face of the capitalist onslaught. Important strikes have broken out in some third world countries, and some of the stronger unions in the developed countries have begun to demand the restitution of their rights. In general, a new epoch of workers' resistance and struggle can be glimpsed worldwide. This struggle is no longer content just to ask for a bigger slice of the pie (wages). It is also seeking to cast doubt on the bosses' right to organize and to manage production within enterprises themselves. Strikes in recent years by US workers in the package delivery industry, of Volkswagen workers in France and Germany, and of Fiat and urban transport workers in Italy point to the renewal of workers' strategies centered on relations of power and control within the workplace itself

Equally important, and a definite strategic advance, is the difficult attempt to reconfigure relations, links, and networks among workers in different sectors of the national economy and among workers internationally. Neoliberalism has made it necessary for struggles to unfold in a global manner. Globalized repression has demanded globalized resistance. The efforts to develop ties among unions in different countries; to organize workers from different "classes" (for example, workers in the first world and subcontracted workers in the third); and to launch resistance campaigns in different parts of the world that bring together social sectors that are distinct but nonetheless equally harmed by neoliberalism (the Battle in Seattle)—all of these efforts, little by little, reveal the possibilities for struggle and resistance under the new conditions of global capitalism.

FRAGMENTATION AND ATOMIZATION

With the introduction of the NEP in Bolivia in 1985, all the centers of production—mining, manufacturing, agriculture, banking, transportation, commerce, services—started to become concentrated in a few hands. That is to say, neoliberalism signaled the enormous privatization of social and natural wealth in each nation and throughout the world. This meant, in turn, that public wealth, whose function was to satisfy collective human needs, was seized by an ambitious minority and converted into a source of private profit. In this way, and under this new model, the Bolivian state began to restructure its functions. No longer does it serve as a capitalist producer itself. It becomes a mere administrator, managing "shared risk" contracts—lease contracts between local enterprises and the transnationals—which allow absolute freedom for the bosses to explore, exploit, market, and enjoy Bolivian wealth.

It is not the case that the state is disappearing—if only that were true! What is happening is that the state has broken away from its older role, when it at least pretended to mediate social contradictions and to redistribute a few crumbs. Now it has shamelessly exposed itself as an efficient servant of big capital, handing it the installations and profits of state-owned enterprises, subsidizing its transportation costs, and, by using repression to guarantee low wages, disciplining its workforce to the new rules of the game.

Paralleling these changes, neoliberalism has disarticulated the large concentrations of highly class-conscious workers seasoned in struggle and has generated new forms of the workforce. The new worker is characterized by fragmentation, individualism, distrust, and submission. This is the result of the growth of small workshops and factories, where workers are not permitted to unionize and are fired at the first sign of an organizing effort. It is further reinforced in the small workshops where children and women labor ten to twelve hours per day without any benefits.

Far from seeing its numbers reduced under neoliberalism, the working class has grown by the thousands and thousands of children and women who have to work for their bread. But this new workforce has remained atomized among an infinity of small businesses, which makes mass struggle difficult. These workers are terrorized by the threat of layoffs or firings; they are vulnerable because they have not yet succeeded in recognizing that their strength lies in unity and struggle. The consciousness of this multitudinous waged and salaried working class still must be constructed.

Class structure in Bolivia, therefore, has been modified in recent years, and the material conditions and features of the working class have been transformed. New forms of class consciousness and solidarity, however, have not yet arisen to match changed conditions and altered workplace identities.

The diverse spaces in which the workforce is concentrated under neoliberalism represent formidable obstacles to working class organization and consciousness. When DS 21060 was imposed in 1985 with its Article 55 on "Free Contract and Hire," many workers were laid off. The bosses took advantage of this moment to downsize their businesses, looking especially to reduce the number of older workers who had both rights and a broad experience in the union movement. These were the workers who were most willing to fight and to resist. Those of us who remain now work in extremely insecure and precarious conditions.

Subsequently, the bosses began to rehire workers, but as temporary laborers, with a contract that permitted only three months' work, during which they earned no seniority.[2] These contract workers did not enjoy the same rights as regular workers and had to perform the hardest work for the lowest wage. This was a strong blow to the unity and strength of the organized labor movement. We regular workers always are mindful of the competition that the temporary workers represent. We feel that we cannot complain about anything or demand any rights, because the boss might immediately fire us and hire one or two of the temporary workers in our place.

As the years went by and the bosses realized how well they were served by the hiring of temporary workers, they began to invent new ways of contracting and subcontracting laborers that resulted in a reorganization of work relations on the shop floor. For example, in many businesses the work process was fragmented by the creation and implementation of "external workshops," in which subcontracted workers would perform part of the production necessary for the final product. The shoe industry provides examples of this "outsourcing." These subcontracted workers labored in especially difficult and harsh conditions in terms of wages, workplace environment, hours, and quotas.

In other enterprises the bosses did not even bother to set up external workshops. Instead, when more workers were needed, the boss would hire new workers through a subcontractor—or recruiter—and the workers would then go to work right on the boss's premises. These workers, who were and are every bit as much "workers" as we are, and who de facto toil for the same boss, were formally hired by somebody else. Because of this technicality they belonged neither to the company nor to the union, and they worked in conditions different (generally worse) from the rest us. All of this meant enormous competition among workers and put great pressure on our job security, rights, and past gains as workers.

In still other businesses, what the bosses have done is to subcontract some production stages to "one-person firms" or to "family enterprises." In these cases what was once done by a regular worker enjoying social security, health benefits, and bonuses is now done by the same worker—but one who has been transformed into a kind of "micro-businessman" laboring under the worst of conditions. That is what has happened, for example, to the workers who distribute and deliver bottled beverages. It has also happened to many maintenance, cleaning, and security workers. In a number of factories, the "micro-business" contracts are for final assembly, and so the worker's whole family gets involved though the whole family does not get paid.

These workers, now disguised as micro or very small-scale "businesspeople," have to accept miserable contracts and possess no rights or job security. In addition, because in the eyes of the law these microbusinesses are the same as the largest enterprises, when a conflict arises they cannot go to the Ministry of Labor to file a grievance.

The forms of hiring and subcontracting are extremely varied, but they all have the same goals: atomizing workers and dividing us against ourselves, taming our resistance and unity, inciting competition among us, and forcing greater productivity per worker at lower wages. This problem of the fragmentation of the Bolivian working class—our dispersion and the variety of working conditions we endure—is the principal problem that Bolivian workers must face up to if we really want to resist, to challenge, and to overcome neoliberalism.

WHAT WE WORKERS CAN NO LONGER DO

Those of us who are still regular waged or salaried workers, who are unionized, and have greater stability in our source of employment, cannot go on thinking that things remain the same as before. Until now, we have mainly acted to resist the bosses' offensive by defending our past gains and hard-won rights. Without a doubt this has been a just struggle. Nevertheless, the time has come for a cold evaluation of the success of that position.

Some of us workers still possess rights and a degree of job security. But we find ourselves constantly pressured by bosses who are out to replace regular workers with temporary ones and to increase productivity. If we resist, they subcontract our jobs out to a workshop where the workers have no rights, and then they turn around and impose on us the same speed-ups anyway. In general, we are on the defensive, without a clear vision or initiative. We watch as each day our past gains are eroded.

A reliable estimate shows that full-time, unionized workers with job security represent only a minority among the gigantic Bolivian working class—the majority of whom are atomized, lacking job security, young, and often silent and desperate. Full-time unionized workers represent only 20 percent of the workforce across the range of economic sectors. The other 80 percent—composed of temporary workers, subcontracted workers, young women, and adolescent boys who are virtually children—labor in conditions where they are completely unprotected, unorganized, and subject to all manner of abuse.[3]

If it is true that some of us can still count on a few rights and benefits, it is also clear what capitalism and the bosses seek to accomplish. They want the total elimination of any possibility of our resistance. They want to convert all workers into disposable parts for their production machine, leaving us no kind of security whatsoever.

On the basis of these elements we can begin to devise the first outlines of a genuine political strategy for Bolivian workers. Our current task is not simply to resist. In the long run, given that we are a minority, and given the pressure of the great mass of temporary and subcontracted workers, we will little by little lose our rights and job security. The only effective way to defend ourselves and launch a real campaign of resistance is to build organizational links to "irregular" workers (and this includes temporaries, subcontracted workers, piecework laborers, and seasonal employees). This strategy needs to encompass every factory, every mine, every enterprise—whether or not it is privatized—and the hundreds of little subcontracting workshops. In other words, it should encompass every workplace. We must realize that the interests of irregular workers are exactly the same as ours. At the moment, because of the bosses' manipulations, it looks like these workers are our competitors. But we are all workers who produce wealth that ends up in the hands of the same bosses. That is why our interests are similar.

It is important to understand that the conditions of class struggle have changed. These are not the good ol' days in which workers were concentrated in great centers of production, and when the government listened if we spoke loud enough. Today the material conditions of work are different, and the ways of struggle are also different. We must convince ourselves of this and begin to discuss current means of resistance and struggle. If not, we will remain on the defensive until we have lost the rights our parents fought so hard to win and which they left us as a legacy.

THE BEGINNING OF A NEW STAGE OF HISTORY

Despite the bosses' offensive, and after twenty years of defeat, frustration, and growing disorganization, Bolivian workers and peasants are demonstrating new social alliances, a recaptured collective dignity, and a revitalized capacity for mobilization.

In Cochabamba and the Aymaran *altiplano*, working men and women, young temporary workers, impoverished neighbors, peasants and townspeople, and unemployed and employed workers have reclaimed the language of the barricades, of community solidarity, and of the assembly and town meeting, in order to make their voices heard. Emerging from the smallest social spaces, previously established neighborhood organizations, newly formed water committees, agrarian unions, and indigenous communities created a powerful network to defend water rights and the traditional practices and uses of water. They took on the state, the police, the military, the bosses, and the politicians. And they won.

As never before during the past twenty years, a people that had united around a people's program and a popular discourse defeated neoliberalism. They tossed a foreign corporation out of the country. Even better, they briefly replaced the government, the political parties, the prefects, and the state itself with a new type of popular government based on assemblies and town meetings held at the regional and state levels. For one week, the state had been demolished. In its place stood the *self-government* of the poor based on their local and regional organizational structures.[4]

These heroic days of April 2000 mark a milestone in the re-constitution of the capacity of the impoverished working classes to mobilize.

WHAT DID WE LEARN?

We learned the importance of uniting all workers on the basis of clear objectives, of having a transparent leadership that shares in the suffering of ordinary people, and of the mass mobilization of workers from both the city and the countryside. With these conditions, it is possible to defeat neoliberal policies, to twist the arm of an indolent state, and to triumph over the false politicians and thieves who have stolen the country's wealth.

Second, the forms of working class unity should not only revolve around the struggle for wages and labor rights but should also encompass, as a fundamental demand, the defense of the basic conditions for life and social reproduction. By this we mean water, land, housing, public services, gas, petroleum, electricity, and all the other basic elements that are necessary for social existence. Neoliberalism wants to privatize these elemental components of life—elements that affect us all, and around which we can unite workers, independent peasants, communal peasants, the unemployed, small businesspeople, townspeople, jobless youth, housewives, and everyone who does not live off someone else's labor. In its voracious drive, neoliberalism is providing us with the means through which we can overcome our fragmentation. There can surface, from this point forward, a new politics of the working classes: the political struggle for the basic necessities of life.

A third lesson is that the organizational forms of the exploited classes and the nations dominated by imperialism are not, nor will they be, solely the trade unions. At the urban level, the trade union as an organizational structure corresponds to the great concentrations of workers who possess indefinite or long-term contracts. Today, the majority of workers are temporary hires and subcontracted laborers, who work for a fixed term in small- and medium-sized businesses. This makes unity based on the workplace difficult to achieve. We must create new union organizations that can bring together workers from individual workplaces and the different trades, and we should group them according to territory or region. This is precisely what the *Coordinadora* in Cochabamba has accomplished in uniting this great multiform torrent of workers, independent peasants, and communal peasants.

This means that, alongside the union-form of organization and mobilization, there will emerge a multitude-form that unites workers from multiple branches of the workforce, with different types of labor contracts, and from both the city and the countryside. The multitude-form is a kind of united front of local, regional, and possibly national masses in which unionized workers and organized peasants can and should assume the lead because of their greater experience in struggle, political clarity, incorruptibility and immediate contact with the rank and file of the movements. In the future, and while the union-form of workers' and popular struggle is being reconstructed, the multitude-form would seem to be the most effective organizational form for uniting popular demands and confronting the state.

Fourth, in the face of neoliberalism, its political parties, and its state, urban and rural workers have begun to build an alternative power and government based on the unification at the state level, and later at the national level, of the neighborhood assemblies, the unions, the peasant communes, and the factories as a network of deliberation, mobilization, and administration of public life. This is precisely what happened in Cochabamba. In the context of a state entrenched in military barracks; of political parties that fled from the scene; of a prefecture, mayoralty, and judicial system that hid inside their homes—there emerged to take power a proud and battle-hardened multitude, a type of self-government based on assemblies and town meetings, in which debates occurred over what should be done with public resources, how to change the laws, and how to defend basic necessities. For the poor in the city and the countryside, the future did not lie in running after city councilors and congresspeople who have privatized and gambled away the public's wealth. The future instead came to consist of communal self-government based on assemblies and town meetings in which all of us are empowered to discuss social issues, where we all decide on our course of action, and where we all take responsibility for putting our decisions into practice.

The final lesson is that workers in general, and factory workers in particular, have proven ourselves capable of raising the banner of national dignity, and of the collective interests of society, by facilitating the unification of generalized popular discontent and single-issue struggles. We factory workers have shown ourselves to be capable of reviving the old role played by Bolivia's miners, who led so many popular struggles and were able to lend them greater resonance and strength. The *Coordinadora* that twisted the arm of the government and set forth a program for popular self-government and a new kind of nation is, without any doubt, a revolutionary creation in which we factory workers have played a vital role through the contribution of our experience, the moral authority we have earned in past struggles, and our ability to elaborate strategic proposals.

The original version of this essay was prepared by Oscar, Raquel, and Álvaro for the Eighteenth Congress of the Confederation of Bolivian Factory Workers, which took place in Oruro during September 2000.

ENDNOTES

1. Larry Elliott and Charlotte Denny, "Top 1% Earn as Much as the Poorest 57%," *The Guardian,* January 18, 2002. http://www.guardian.co.uk/business/story/0,3604,635292,00.html (September 2004).
2. Workers can be hired on a temporary basis for up to three months. In Bolivia, these workers are called *eventuales.* Under existing labor law, after three months' employment *eventuales* become regular, indefinitely contracted workers with guaranteed benefits. The normal business practice, however, is to fire such workers at the end of their short-term contracts and then rehire them for another three months—keeping them as non-unionized labor paid at extremely low wages.
3. Iriarte, *Análisis Crítico de la Realidad,* 379.
4. The "state" in question here is the government of the State of Cochabamba. The national government of the Republic of Bolivia did not collapse and was not replaced during the Water War.

FOR A CONSTITUENT ASSEMBLY
CREATING PUBLIC SPACES

It was in September—at a city-wide meeting held in the Plaza 14 de Septiembre—that the slogan "For a Constituent Assembly" emerged. People demanded an assembly where we could rebuild the country from the bottom—from the position of those excluded by the present system, from the neighborhoods and communities.

Since democracy was conquered during the 1980s, Bolivia has suffered changes that directly affect the organizations of civil society, the economic base, and the political and social relations of all of us who live in this country.

The slow weakening of the *Central Obrera Boliviana* (COB; Bolivian Workers Confederation) and the change in production has filled the lives of the majority of Bolivians with uncertainty, vulnerability, and increasingly precarious work conditions. The privatization of national enterprises has never generated the incomes that were promised. On the contrary, privatization has meant the total loss of sovereignty and control over natural resources. At the same time it has led to an increase in the cost of living and basic services.

A similar process has occurred in the national congress and the city councils, which have been turned into "private" spaces under the almost exclusive control of the political parties. Political participation and decision-making is limited to spaces designed by the parties and lacking in content—which they then attempt to pass off as "deliberation" and "dialogue."

OSCAR OLIVERA

The Bolivian state—the new state that has been taking shape since 1985—is a state that listens only to itself. It is an authoritarian state that dissembles and negates the possibility of real deliberation. For genuine discussion to occur, a mutual recognition among social actors is necessary. Yet in the cities and the countryside, in the eyes of ordinary working people, the state and private enterprise are completely discredited. So, too, are the intellectuals who justify, in the name of "governability," their self-serving and self-proclaimed political class. The political class has made the country its fiefdom, and it has lost its value as a social actor.

Every day we watch defenseless as the corruption and impunity of the political system parades before our eyes in the media. No matter what the form, the government has almost always ruled behind the backs of the people. But what interests the people is the content of the government. During the past twenty years, the state apparatus has been administered directly by the business class, what could be called the different sectors of the Bolivian elite. The business class of every party stripe has, in turn, applied neoliberal economic policies with the results that we all know. Legislative power is the expression of an elitist representative democracy—and, as such, has always responded to the interests of the dominant classes.

What has occurred and continues to occur—this must be underlined—is that a larger and larger strata of people are becoming conscious of the reactionary, cynical, and corrupt nature of the national congress. We have begun to identify congressional members by what they do and not by what they say. The uprisings starting with the Water War have stripped naked before everyone the true identity of the different congressional "brigades." They all allied against the people. They all sought to confuse, to trick, and to deceive the people by giving free rein to their verbal juggling acts.

In response, people are discovering new public spaces for discussion and debate. Today the principal context for deliberation is no longer the organized trade union movement, as it was prior to 1985. Deliberation—which for us encompasses expressing opinion, debating, deciding, and putting into practice—now occurs in the new world of labor that the *modelo*, or neoliberalism, has created. During April 2000 in Cochabamba and May 2000 in La Paz, it was workers from the informal sector, as one social researcher named them, who took over space, who took control of time, and above all who seized the power to speak.

Conflict is not a disease. To a certain extent it is good, because it allows us to open spaces for discussion, so we can see ourselves, so we can recognize ourselves, so we can speak among ourselves, and so we can begin truly to become "the people." Other public spaces—such as the official councils, the congress, the courts, the prefectures, the Government Palace—no longer serve us, and maybe they never did.

The people have opened their own spaces—in the streets, in the road blockades, in the neighborhood assemblies, in the town meetings, in the coalitions—in order to entwine their solidarity, to collectively and mutually raise their spirits and morale, and to rescue their values. With their actions, with their desires, with their fears, with their unity, and with their organization, the people are beginning to forge a new kind of democracy. This democracy is neither delegated nor representative, but authentic, participatory, direct, and without intermediaries. It is a democracy in which deliberation occurs among equals in order later to break out into action.

Discussions were held about the water law in the congress, in the name of the people, until the people turned away from that space, because it corresponds to a devalued and usurped democracy. It is a fraudulent space. That is why the people took their discussion of a mercantile and confiscatory water law to Cochabamba. There the law was changed through the people's mobilization. There deliberative spaces made possible the expulsion of a transnational corporation that had assumed power over our water system by means of a completely irregular and opaque process. Faced with the deafness, blindness, and obstinacy of the authorities and the "duly constituted" organizations, people opted to construct their own legitimate instruments and their own arenas for discussion, decision, and execution of their demands.

This was not limited to the water issue. Fundamentally, people began to understand that the content of their spaces of deliberation—the true content of their demands—was essentially their position about their own living conditions, about the way the country had dismantled the patrimony of their natural resources.

It was about how people felt trampled down, ignored, deprecated, excluded, and dispossessed of their most basic rights as citizens and workers. In such circumstances people began to talk, to communicate with each other, and to regain confidence in themselves and in their neighbors. They began to unite, organize, and feel solidarity. They began to lose their fear. They demanded to be heard and to be taken seriously. Their demands were no longer limited to changing a law or getting rid of the transnationals but grew instead to encompass a demand for justice—for full social justice. And this demand is difficult, if not impossible, to perceive from behind a desk, from a congressional seat, from a police station, or from a military barrack.

This conflict has made it possible for ordinary people to understand not only that things must change in our country but also that they can be changed. We have left behind the tutelage of the political parties in regard to decision-making. We have begun to decide things from below, and our desires have become reality. More than patching up or repairing the *modelo,* we are attempting the necessary genuine transformations in decision-making and in the ways democracy is conducted.

What worries us the most is that the politicians, the business leaders, and those intellectuals who think they are the owners of public speech, of public opinion, of "legitimate" solutions, and of the "institutions of democracy" do not realize, and do not want to realize, that the people have begun to think and act for themselves. If our messages and signals are not perceived with absolute clarity by those who, until now, have governed and thought for us, we will soon enter a violent and uncontrollable resolution of our conflicts. This was seen when, during the Water War, the government sent sharpshooters because the people began to decide things for themselves—because the "Indians" and the savages were expressing their ideas, taking decisions, and putting them into practice.

Given this panorama, will we be in a position to create spaces and to reach agreements for resolving conflicts within the framework of this democracy? Sometimes we are very pessimistic, but we recognize that the country has begun to change after April 2000. Everyone recognizes this—some with fear and panic, others with hope and confidence. With our eyes, ears, and lips, ordinary working people have found a path toward building a new democracy.

¡COCHABAMBA!

THE CONSTITUENT ASSEMBLY

One response to the crisis that envelops our country is the call for a Constituent Assembly put forward by the *Coordinadora,* which is being discussed everywhere—in the neighborhoods, the universities, and the streets. We have proposed a Constituent Assembly because we believe that solving the crisis involves more than just changing the head of government. We must go further and fundamentally change the rules of the game. We need a space where the people can talk not about the past, but the future. For this reason we are proposing a Constituent Assembly in which all of society can participate in designing its own country.

In order to analyze the pros and cons of a Constituent Assembly in Bolivia, we should start by considering the moment in which the proposal is being made and ask why is it being proposed at this time. And the answer surfaces of its own accord in light of the acute economic crisis caused by neoliberalism, which has only globalized poverty and unemployment.

Recent conflicts have shown that the Bolivian people not only seek to satisfy specific demands but also to find longer-term solutions. We know that a change brought about by elections would not mean a significant transformation for the country. It is evident to everyone that the return to our current democracy has only served as a social ladder for the political class. All that has changed has been the alliances among parties in the divvying up of quotas of power. In keeping with the plans of the IMF and other international organizations, neoliberal economic policy has continued throughout. The servants have changed, but the menu is always the same.

The liberal perspective is that poor people should devote themselves to work—to plowing, to making shoes, to growing lettuce—because politics is for the enlightened. In other words, people are only good for votes and not for their ideas about daily realities. But we say, "No, that's not true!"

A new democracy is being built by the people who are no longer, and can no longer be, satisfied by a delegated or representative democracy. Emerging from the united actions of people and the voicing of their desires and fears is an authentic, participatory, and direct democracy. In these spaces and organizations deliberation—discussion, decision, and implementation—takes place without intermediaries and between equals. We believe that the reconstitution of the popular movement on the basis of solidarity is something that is under way and cannot be stopped.

The Constituent Assembly, brought into being by and for the people, is only an instrument toward realizing needed changes. We do not believe that it is the only solution, because there is no recipe for solving the crisis. Nevertheless, at the present time, it represents the only concrete proposal and the only alternative put forward to deal with the crisis. It can be a beginning.

In April 2000 people embarked on a search for solutions that took them beyond the framework of the market. In this search we are discovering new forces and new social actors with positive political creativity. Above all, we are discovering tremendous solidarity in the face of the problems we share.

THE QUEST TO RECOVER DEMOCRACY

In the middle of the conflicts of September 2000, when a multitude of struggles were being waged across Bolivia, the *Coordinadora* proposed the call for a Constituent Assembly as one of its slogans. Although the call had been raised before by others, it has acquired importance today as a result of the social cataclysm from which it emerged and the fact that thousands and thousands of mobilized citizens have adopted it as a practical orientation.

The politicians and the right-wing intellectuals wasted no time in responding to defend the status quo. Appealing to arguments about "preserving democracy," and pointing out that no provision exists for a Constituent Assembly in Bolivian law, they devoted themselves to expressing not only their disagreement with, but their total opposition to, any kind of discussion that would open a debate over the rules of the game that presently organize the country's political life.

Nevertheless, if the recent demonstrations have revealed anything, it is the will of the population to recover the capacity to decide in public affairs and on any issue that involves the collective interest. The Water War in Cochabamba mobilized tens of thousands of people who, in a public and collective process, decided not to accept the handing over of the city's water service to a transnational corporation. The deep meaning of this struggle, in the eyes of the protagonists themselves, resides in the refusal to acquiesce to a governmental decision that we perceived as arbitrary, unjust, and wrong.

Beyond the indignation over the rate hikes, or the threat that the collectively built neighborhood wells would be confiscated, the slogans *"Aguas del Tunari* Get Out!" and "No to the Law on Drinking Water and Sewers" showed the overwhelming determination of Cochabamba's inhabitants to participate in public affairs. They consciously aimed to erode the monopoly on political decision-making which, in the form of an exclusionist and partisan "democracy," had been imposed as the norm.

Once the withdrawal of *Aguas del Tunari* was achieved and the contract rescinded, the fundamental questions of politics remained on the discussion table: How are decisions going to be made? In what way will the notion of the "common good" be constructed? Beyond the actual discussion of what form the new water company might assume in Cochabamba, what occurred and continues to take place is that people are looking for ways to intervene collectively in public affairs. In other words, people are searching for a way to turn politics into a patrimony of the citizenry and not just of a vile caste.

These facts should be kept in mind when analyzing the proposal for a Constituent Assembly that came out of Cochabamba. In the first place, they attest to a thick social fabric made up of associations, committees, and groups with common interests and autonomous means of solving collective problems. In the second place, they show us an experience of managing public affairs in a specific area—the distribution of water—that has proven successful and is serving to rebuild people's confidence in their ability to see to their own needs.

Questioning governmental decisions, criticizing the exclusionary form of decision-making, perceiving the exercise of power as a series of arbitrary acts—these are the elements which have set the stage for the generalization of a collective will to recover democracy as the direct running of society in the common interest. This collective will expresses itself in the proposal for a Constituent Assembly.

It is compelling that this slogan restores a link to the historic struggle for the conquest of democracy, insofar as it indicts the current expropriation of our voices and the monopoly of public decision-making by the political parties. It emphasizes this link even more by insisting on the collective participation of society in the decision-making process and in the design of the forms of the country's political organization.

The proposal for a Constituent Assembly embodies the virtue of giving a non-party content to the social movement of the past few years. By allowing the people's mobilization to develop a horizon beyond the immediate interest of a salary increase or land title, and beyond the immediate question of drinking water or irrigation, it enables a non-party space of discussion over what should be the "common good" or "collective interest"—that is, the desirable form of our collective life. Moreover, the slogan promotes inclusiveness, for it calls out to urban workers, irrigation farmers, villagers, *cocaleros,* Aymaran communities, landless peasants, and beyond. Indeed, the slogan aims to generate a space of encounter for all these sectors of society, in which, together, they can design an acceptable way of coexisting and of finding solutions to the most serious problems faced by each group.

The Constituent Assembly presents itself as a new type of political action born out of civil society as a means to discuss and to decide collective matters. We must determine the distinct meanings attributed to the proposal, since—quite correctly—the manner in which it is implemented will define its potential for social transformation. What is the Constituent Assembly? Who calls it into being? How should it be organized? In the answers to these questions there can surface differences which will determine whether the Constituent Assembly results in "a supreme moment of democracy" or in mere agreements among "experts" who once again will exclude the citizenry from decision-making power.

For the *Coordinadora,* the Constituent Assembly is basically an instance of the political organization of civil society. Through it, working men and women recover the ability to participate in, to discuss, and to decide collective issues in a direct manner, without intermediaries, and without the patronage of "advisors" or "experts."

The Constituent Assembly thus should be understood as a great sovereign meeting of citizen representatives elected by their neighborhood organizations, their urban or rural associations, their unions, their communes. These citizen representatives would bring with them ideas and projects concerning how to organize the political life of the country. They would seek to define the best way of organizing and managing the common good, the institutions of society, and the means that could unite the different individual interests in order to form a great collective and national interest. They would decide upon the modes of political representation, social control, and self-government that we should give ourselves for the ensuing decades. And all of these agreed decisions would immediately be implemented. In this way, the kind of Constituent Assembly we propose is a sovereign power that depends on no one other than those who provide its mandate—in this case, the society of urban and rural workers, organized according to its customs and practices, its unions, and its associations. It is a supreme temporal authority that defines for the long term the national organization of citizens' lives and political presence.

The Constituent Assembly is a form of recovering and exercising political sovereignty, that is, of gaining the capacity to make and to execute public policy. This capacity is currently mortgaged to the system of political parties. The Constituent Assembly, therefore, is not based on the reform of the political constitution of the existing state. The Constituent Assembly does not seek to become the government, but to create the space where the people can decide their own future. It recovers the very first premise of a republic: "Sovereignty resides in the people." In this way it sets in motion a general transformation of political institutions to correct the present situation of exclusions and lack of recognition for the political rights of the citizenry.

THE RELEVANCE OF A CONSTITUENT ASSEMBLY

Given that the current system of political parties has demonstrated its incapacity to represent society, it seems pertinent to think, to discuss, and to construct other forms of internal political organization for society in order to confront common issues. The political parties have become closed cliques of people who limit themselves to taking care of their own interests and pursuing from their state offices all kinds of private business ventures. Moreover, the only way in which the political parties link up with working-class society is through the exchange of favors, bribes, and the buying and selling of votes. No mechanisms exist to stimulate the participation of the population in decision-making. Rather, the mechanisms that do exist ensure, in one way or another, that it remains impossible for the population to express its viewpoints and to pursue its demands and necessities as public policies.

In the face of this reality, the Constituent Assembly becomes a mechanism for civil reorganization in order to take charge of the direction of public affairs. It is precisely in the manner of carrying out such an experience of reorganization, however, that the different positions surrounding the Constituent Assembly begin to distinguish themselves. Is it to be understood as an autonomous act of social unification, or is it to be converted into a kind of demand for reform addressed to the existing government? In the latter case, the transformative potential of the Constituent Assembly would be diluted.

In our view, an authentic Constituent Assembly emerges from a call by the autonomous organizations of ordinary working people to bring together other social sectors. The Constituent Assembly is a deliberative and executive body which discusses the most urgent needs facing everyone and agrees upon ways of responding to those needs. Within the Assembly representatives of active rank-and-file organizations gather together in order to discuss their own needs and to develop proposals for resolving them. They discover ways of unifying their needs and political proposals with the needs and proposals of other sectors.

In other words, the Constituent Assembly is a great laboratory in which the political future of the nation is shaped for the coming decades on the basis of the initiatives, demands, and proposals of all citizens who assume responsibility for the construction of the common good. For this very reason, it is not a gathering of marginal specialists or lawyers seeking a niche in the political caste. As we conceive of it, the Constituent Assembly spells the death of the political caste, of the specialists, and of the monopolists of the power of speech.

The Constituent Assembly is not a reunion of complaints and demands, nor is it simply the presentation of what each group, sector, or community desires. It is a place, above all, where the distinct sectors of organized society propose to the others a means of coexistence—of living together, of organizing and ordering collective experience. As such, the Constituent Assembly requires that prior collective discussions and processes of unification and internal organization have taken place in the communities, neighborhoods, unions, and indigenous communities. This strengthening of local political life allows the democratic development of concrete proposals concerning how to organize the country, its territory, and the political system for future years.

The reorganization of working-class society is a process that has scarcely begun. Examples of the reorganization can be seen in the *Confederación Sindical Unica de Trabajadores Campesinos de Bolivia* (CSUTCB; Confederation of Bolivian Peasant Workers), which has rebuilt the communal fabric of the *altiplano* in particular, and the *Coordinadora*. Other regions and other sectors of labor throughout the country are strengthening their capacity to mobilize—a strengthening which will equip them to engage in the discussion over how to organize the political life of the country. Hence, the call for a true Constituent Assembly, outside of the discredited government, can be a mobilizing issue for the next months and years. And the Constituent Assembly itself will be the fruit of a process of rearticulating social movements and collective struggles on a national scale.

Let us be clear: Neither the executive branch nor the legislative branch, not even the political parties, can convoke the Constituent Assembly. These institutions and their members all stand discredited for having plunged the country into disaster. The Constituent Assembly will be convoked by society itself which, organized and mobilized, is ready to assume responsibility for taking the country's political destiny into its own hands.

The Constituent Assembly has been proposed by the most active and compact organizations of society, such as the *Coordinadora,* the Irrigators' Federation, the *Fabriles,* and various neighborhood associations. The next step is for other grassroots rank-and-file organizations—ones with the same capacity for self-organization and the same commitment to a future with dignity—to also take up this proposal, to amplify it, to enrich it, and to publicize it. In this way, a great network of organizations can take shape in the middle term. And these organizations can carry out the self-convocation of the entire population so that together they may produce the new citizenry that will direct the collective political destiny of the country.

TOWARD A NATIONAL AND CONTINENTAL REBELLION

One lesson of the Water War in Cochabamba stands out clearly: the need to dismantle the existing state. The Bolivian state has functioned over the last twenty years as the agent of neoliberalism. It has served the interests of an international and national elite who have enriched themselves at the expense of the needs and interests of ordinary working people. In order to end this exploitation, we need to create a real democracy, one that works from below and allows for the full participation, deliberation, and decision-making of the population. Such a new kind of state can come into existence only through the united action of the various social movements. Achieving this unity, however, requires greater consciousness and greater organization than we have at present.

AN ATTEMPT AT NATIONAL UNITY

In April 2001—a year after the Water War—the *Coordinadora* took an initial step to create greater unity among the various sectors of society that had come out in protest of the government. These dispersed sectors, each with their individual demands, included the *cocaleros*, people of the *altiplano*, small debtors, pensionless workers, artisans, self-employed, transportation workers, landless squatters, peasants from every region, and indigenous peoples. In the midst of Cochabamba's Water War in April 2000, we had already conceived the idea of an *Estado Mayor del Pueblo* (EMP; People's Joint Chiefs of Staff) for the social movement. We thus launched a call for a national meeting to pull together a single national bloc, and, in April 2001, we formed the *Coordinadora de Movilizaciones Única Nacional* (COMUNAL; Coalition for National Mobilizations), which included the groups mentioned above, as well as ourselves—the *Coordinadora, Fabriles,* and others—in Cochabamba.

COMUNAL was founded on April 7, and we immediately launched into a national march that began April 9. Our demands focused primarily on the issues of coca, water, land, and a solution to the problems of small debtors. A large number of workers who had bid successfully on state housing, but later discovered they had been cheated and were now demanding compensation, also participated.

Another march had served as a preamble to the one called for April 9. The earlier march began on March 20 and was led by the *Central Obrera Departamental—Cochabamba* (COD; Cochabamba State Federation of Workers) after the national *Central Obrera Boliviana* (COB; Confederation of Bolivian Workers) had refused to mobilize. We marched in support of the different sectional demands, but we sought primarily to call attention to the fact that the only way to get out of Bolivia's economic crisis was to reclaim the enterprises that the government had privatized. Here we were concerned with the large, formerly state-owned enterprises such as *Yacimientos Petrolíferos Fiscales Bolivianos* (oil wells and refineries), *Lloyd Aéreo Boliviano* (airlines), ENFE (railways), ENDE (electric power), and everything related to telecommunications, electricity, and hydrocarbons.

The March 20 action drew a small column of scarcely thirty workers. The government repressed it harshly, arresting us and leaving the march with twenty-six men and women. Two hundred police and forty government agents spread out along the highway and followed us more than 200 kilometers—and all because the *Coordinadora* and I were supposedly in the march. The government claimed that we wanted to call attention to ourselves. Of course, we did want to call attention to the theme of the march; we never pretended to do anything else. The theme—the march to recover the homeland—was a threat because it emphasized that the country had been alienated from ordinary working people and that it had been given away as a gift to foreign interests.

Since we had been forced to cut short the earlier march, we started out the April 9 mobilization to La Paz with a very large presence—some one thousand men and women. The government was more worried this time and did everything it could to ensure that the march would fail to win the support of important sectors of the population. A number of social organizations, including the COB, agreed with the government's assertion that the march was "political," in the sense that it aimed only to increase the political power of the *cocaleros* and the *Coordinadora* through projecting a kind of parallel or dual unionism. Curiously, the COB was much harder in its criticisms of the march than the government was.

The police tried to break up the march seven times during its trajectory. About a fourth of the way to La Paz several of us were arrested—the march had split up into three columns, and the police saw this maneuver as a threat to their ability to exercise control. One column stayed on the highway, but the other two continued on footpaths through the hills and mountains.

The first attack by the government occurred approximately 80 kilometers outside of Cochabamba. They took us prisoner and brought us to an isolated place on the outskirts of the city. We thought maybe they intended to kill us—it was night and very dark, and there was a huge police presence. That did not happen, so two days later we rejoined the march. We had walked only a few kilometers when the government intervened again with tanks, helicopters, and a large number of soldiers. The march then split once more into several columns as a strategy for getting to La Paz.

The march continued for several more days, with much sacrifice and effort on the part of the participants to fulfill their objective of reaching La Paz simply to be heard. We workers demanded job security, and other sectors voiced their most important demands. There were also many young people on the march. In the evenings, when we rested and could talk among each other, each group began to learn about the conditions and struggles of the others. We could all feel a tremendous solidarity awakening and taking hold. Back on the road, what most struck me was the support from the people through whose villages we passed. Some of the villages had no electricity or clear means of communication to the outside, but they all knew that we were marching to La Paz and why. At every step we were the recipients of amazing solidarity. The peasant communities of the *altiplano* gave us food and lodging. They guided us through the mountains, showing us shortcuts, and we finally arrived at El Alto, the elevated city of the poor adjacent to La Paz, thanks to these communities and our own perseverance.

Although it fell short of immediately cementing the kind of unity we sought, the COMUNAL march in 2001 did succeed in articulating our demands. It became part of a slow process of reconstituting solidarity and projecting a united social movement. In 2000 and 2001 it was the social movements which set the agendas of national debate. It was not the parliamentarians, the businessmen, or the government who set the agenda. The social movements consistently defined the arena of debate, and I believe that they will go on doing so. The major headlines in the newspapers and television media were never about this or that proposal to amend some law in the National Congress. Rather, they reflected the demands for tractors and land, the struggle of the *cocaleros,* the fight for water rights—and, ominously, the growing number of deaths in the struggle for social justice.

REPRESSION SPURS UNITY

What drove us to march on La Paz was and is quite specific and real: the privatization of our national enterprises throughout all of Latin America has converted us into exporters of dollars, that is, exporters of the very wealth we generate within our own borders. Consider electric power in Cochabamba, for example. Of the money we pay for electricity, barely 12 percent goes into lighting for the public, and another 13 percent stays here in the form of taxes. Practically all of the rest is hauled away by foreign interests, since the distribution, transportation, and so forth are all in the hands of transnational companies. Nothing of our own wealth is left for the country. The same thing occurs with hydrocarbons. For every dollar Bolivia produces, hardly six cents stays here, and this means that the Bolivian state increasingly possesses fewer means to satisfy the demands of the population. There is less circulation of money and, hence, less consumption.

This robbery by the transnationals, with the aid of their accomplices among the Bolivian elite, constitutes the material basis of our shared experiences. It creates the potential for our real unity and solidarity.

An atmosphere of complete insecurity defines the existence of people in Bolivia. In the marketplaces, there are seas of young people and abandoned children who have no jobs, and who have no choice but to steal. I believe that, among our people, it is more dignified to rob than beg. After all, our government officials and business leaders regularly travel abroad with their hands held out begging for spare change from the US and other countries. People notice the way they act. Our people want to fight for their right to good living conditions. They want to fight against poverty, not beg for charity. I think it really is better to steal the wallet of some congressperson than to beg.

The economic situation in Bolivia—where we are headed—has become unviable. There will not be a reactivation of the country's productive apparatus; there will be no job creation; and there will be no improvement of peoples' lives under current conditions. The government has tried many things over the years to obtain immediate resources—granting housing support, monetizing the stocks of the privatized companies, seeking a way to ensure a *Bolivida* (a small annual bonus) for retirees and the elderly—all as a way of injecting new money into the economy and as a way of seeking to placate a restless population. One reason for the government's plan to sell natural gas to the transnationals at outrageously low prices has been precisely to obtain money right away. Being desperate, it believes that it is in too weak a position to negotiate terms favorable to the whole nation.

I believe that the economists and those who think they can become the masters of power over the next few years will realize that this country has no way out under present conditions. Now there is nothing big left for them to rob; the great robberies occurred when the *Movimiento Nacionalista Revolucionario* (MNR; Nationalist Revolutionary Movement) privatized our companies, when the politicians just surrendered them for an unbelievable pittance in a completely immoral and antipatriotic manner. With no big thefts left to pull, the government merely steals on the cheap: running contraband meat, selling bureaucratic posts, laying surcharges on vaccinations and public health campaigns. They have become vulgar pickpockets. Since there is no more money, the politicians cannot be bank robbers, and so they devote themselves to mugging pedestrians.

But the misery they inflict upon us and the sense of hopelessness they spawn within us simultaneously create our common interest. Misery and despair nourish, if not our bellies, our dreams of a powerful unity.

Economic theft is not the only force bearing down on us in recent years. Military repression has also intensified under neoliberalism. Especially after 9/11 in the US, the sacrifices endured by ordinary working Bolivians have become much greater. Bolivia's first two post-9/11 presidents, Jorge Quiroga and Gonzalo Sánchez de Lozada, adopted a language and a vocabulary that were more aggressive than even George W. Bush's. What was particularly troubling was that Quiroga indicated at a White House meeting in Washington, DC, that he would not allow drug trafficking or terrorism to hide behind the "so-called social movements." This statement clearly announced Quiroga's intention to criminalize and to crack down on the peasant movement, the *cocalero* movement, and citizen movements in general. During Quiroga's first four months in office, there were twenty deaths. The government's attitude took a virtually fascist turn under Quiroga, in my opinion.

The departure of General Hugo Banzer from the presidency in August 2001 raised many people's hopes, given the youth of his successor, Quiroga, and his distance from the Banzer dictatorship. But we have always maintained that Quiroga is one of the best students of the neoliberal model and that the composition of his cabinet indicated he intended to apply the *modelo* with ever greater "efficiency."

Banzer's economic crew had proven completely inefficient in administering the *modelo;* many things escaped their control. But Quiroga's new economic team knew what it was doing. And this meant they did not care about preserving the national base of our industries, or about overseeing the operations and accounting of the privatized businesses, or about maintaining the purchasing power of ordinary working people's salaries and wages, or about inflation, or about the effects of external debt on our standard of living. Hence, in the face of any protest, the government automatically called out the army and deployed police in the streets. The subsequent government of Sánchez de Lozada has continued this practice.

This aggression emanates from a political system and a state apparatus that were and still are totally corrupt and discredited in the eyes of the population. The political circle—the presidents, the police, the parliamentarians, and the business community—has fallen into disrepute because of favoritism and greed. But what most irritates the population, what causes the greatest indignation, is the cynicism with which this elite band of individuals acts. They think we are all stupid and that we will just accept their deals and their nepotism.

I often thought that if a popular revolt were to occur in Bolivia like the one in Argentina in December 2001, it would not be mainly because of hunger, as it was in Argentina, but because of indignation. People want to say "Enough!" to all these corrupt figures who think the populace is stupid. Bolivians would not raid a supermarket; they would burn down the National Congress. And that is virtually what happened here, when the people set fire to government buildings in La Paz and El Alto during the tax war of February 2003.

A JOINT CHIEFS OF STAFF

The collapse of the Argentine economy following the sell-off of Argentina's industries in the 1990s, like the present situation here in Bolivia, shows that the world economy views Latin American countries only as a source of profits to be vacuumed up. The bosses' surrender to foreigners of our wealth, our enterprises, and our natural resources ought to unite all Latin Americans. There is no other alternative.

While the people are generously sacrificing their lives in struggle—thirty dead in the *Argentinazo*, eighty dead in the Bolivian Gas War—the elites continue to hold power. It is not a question of simply changing the personalities in power. It is a matter of changing the *modelo,* the economic structure of society, in order to bring about a more equal distribution of wealth. It is also a matter of changing the political structure to let people participate in decision-making and be accountable for public acts. Without such changes, I believe that we are on the verge of even greater struggles in our countries.

As early as the Water War, we had conceived the idea of an EMP as a way to provide direction and coordination for the social struggle. The Bolivian EMP finally formed out of the coca war of January 2003. Some of the sectors represented included the *cocaleros,* the Urban Teachers Union, the State Confederations of Factory Workers, and the *Coordinadora*. Our aim was to bring greater unity into the movement in order to allow our struggles and actions to prove more effective.

The EMP was not up to our first tests, however. The February 2003 "tax revolt" took us by surprise. Again, no group was able to channel the popular discontent into a decisive blow against neo-liberalism. Nor did we play a significant role in the October 2003 Gas War. The people's actions unfolded in a largely spontaneous manner until the very end, when the succession of Vice President Carlos Mesa was negotiated. The current context of the Gas War makes maintaining the original Bolivian EMP difficult. Its leaders are divided on the best strategy to pursue in attempting to recover hydrocarbon resources for the Bolivian people.

Despite all of this, I still believe in the importance of creating and developing an effective EMP in Bolivia. And I believe that the *Coordinadora* has a central role to play in shaping a viable EMP. For as long as the *Coordinadora* has the possibility of maintaining contact with the population; for as long as it can serve as a voice of the population; for as long as it is identified with people's aspirations; for as long as it remains honest and does what it says it will do; and for as long as it genuinely listens to people—then it can serve as a force to bring people together and to mobilize their energies.

Beyond the necessity of national and continental unity, there is another dimension of struggle that the creation of EMPs must address. 9/11 has given the United States a huge pretext for criminalizing protest and dissent. When the interests of the corporations and imperialism are threatened, the US will intervene in Latin America. Our own governments will do their master's bidding and invite the US to intervene. All of our governments are, at bottom, the same: business, political, military, and even religious elites who are neoliberalism junior partners.

AN INTERNATIONAL STRUGGLE

There exists a future for the coming together of the different social movements in Bolivia. More than anything else, however, I believe that it is crucial to strengthen the fronts of struggle in each and every country of Latin America. Neoliberalism and the national governments have worked to divide, fragment, and pulverize the social movements. Yet globalization has also globalized the conditions of resistance, of struggle, and of people's hardship.

All over Latin America, as in Bolivia, the social movements are dispersed, and significant mistrust exists among them. How can unity and solidarity be built in each country, and across the continent?

Based on our experience in Cochabamba, people can try to find in each country, community, and neighborhood a problem or issue that can unite people—something that can lead people to lose their fear and to take decisions on their own. I believe that the social movements, their leaders, and their militants must discover the guiding threads that can pull people together.

Furthermore, the possibility must exist for people to believe in something. Nowadays people do not believe in anything; they feel used, abused, and deceived. I consider that the *Coordinadora* has given Cochabambinos something to believe in, something they know will not betray them. I believe that this is really important.

Social fighters across the continent also need to develop the ability to listen to people. Left-wing leaders often prefer to hear themselves talk rather than listen to others. But we have to know how to listen—and to be able to do so all the time. I have met people in various countries with an extraordinary capacity for analysis, and for knowing what people want. But I have also encountered organizations in these same countries that talk big but are terribly bureaucratized. Their leaders keep talking about socialism as the only alternative, as if socialism were just around the corner. But if you say this in a neighborhood today, people will call you a "traditional politician"—not because they do not believe in socialism, but rather because they would say, "What I want right now is that the city politicians stop robbing me in order to pay for the sewers." People want this kind of thing first, and then we can discuss socialism.

People want to participate, intervene, and hold the politicians accountable. They are tired of the rich stealing not only their money but also their rights—their rights as individuals to speak, to express opinions, to dissent, to form a union. I believe that we have to start from people's daily problems in order to advance to more general questions.

There exists fear among the ruling classes of the Latin American nations today. We must prepare ourselves both to take advantage of it and to defend ourselves against reactions based on it. We must learn to listen rather than to preach to ordinary working people in order to understand their conditions and hopes. We must create new components of the social struggle, such as the EMPs, that can develop greater unity among the social movements. Above all, we need to understand our struggle against neoliberalism as an international one—as a struggle in which the fates of ordinary Bolivians or Argentines or Ecuadorians or Venezuelans or Brazilians, as well as the peoples of every Latin American nation, remain crucially interdependent.

This chapter is drawn from interviews conducted in January 2002. At the time, Jorge Quiroga was President of Bolivia, having succeeded as Vice President to the presidency following the resignation of President Hugo Banzer for health reasons in summer 2001. The perspectives put forward in the chapter apply, perhaps even more forcefully, to conditions under the present government of President Gonzalo Sánchez de Losada, who was elected in 2002 and driven from office in 2003.

¡THE GAS WAR!

PETROLEUM AND NATURAL GAS
RECONQUERING OUR COLLECTIVE PATRIMONY

Petroleum and natural gas are riches found in our territory; they represent national wealth. The presence of oil and gas provides an objective condition that can permit the expansion of the national economy and the raising of the quality of life and work using our own Bolivian resources. Bolivia possesses a great wealth of petroleum and natural gas, but these resources do not currently benefit the Bolivian people. Despite the current situation, these deposits are important for the future economic viability of Bolivia.

The sheer value of the oil and gas is important to the future of the Bolivian economy. The 52.3 trillion cubic feet of gas reserves in Bolivia—reserves presently in the hands of foreign capitalists—are minimally worth $120 billion.[1] This means that financial resources exist in Bolivia for improving the living conditions of the whole population. The resources exist for job creation, better salaries, and expanding free services.

One hundred twenty billion dollars is an extraordinary amount of money. Such funds can enable the creation of a new productive base that could halt the country's decline and rescue it from industrial and commercial insignificance. The resources exist to modify the structure of national production by broadening its industrial base, improving the transportation system, and diversifying the economy. Better yet, it could build the economy without the foreign loans or favors that always end up submerging us in greater dependency.

But as long as this wealth belongs to foreign businessmen who have appropriated resources that belong to others, these dreams remain unfulfilled. Foreign capitalists are getting rich, and intend to go on getting rich, from these resources. They restrict the possibilities that this wealth, which should belong to us, might be used to benefit the lives of all Bolivians. The capitalists, whether local or foreign, puts profits and her or his own personal benefit above the collective and national interest. The transfer of wealth to private and foreign hands is the fate that has befallen the collective national patrimony.

What could be a source of rebirth for the productive capacity of the nation is, for now, only a source of profits and private fortunes for a handful of capitalists. The private ownership of petroleum and natural gas by these businessmen constitutes, without any doubt, the strangulation of one of the greatest opportunities the nation has ever had to finance and to sustain the type of productive growth that can benefit the population, satisfy our needs, and fulfill our right to a dignified communal life.

We have economic wealth, but this wealth is not under our control. We have the potential to make a great technological and productive leap that could benefit working people—the real owners of the gas and oil. Yet those who stand ready to benefit are foreign businessmen and their local commercial and political associates who have handed over to foreign capital what belongs not to them but to all Bolivians.

Bolivia's possession of natural gas and petroleum, because of their world-wide use, is what most strongly ties the national economy to world trade and foreign investment. The principal consumers of Bolivia's hydrocarbons are businesses, governments, and citizens of other nations, particularly those in neighboring countries. Moreover, it is estimated that by the end of 2000 direct gas-related foreign investment in Bolivia originating from extremely powerful multinational companies will total $1.4 billion, equivalent to 20 percent of our GDP.[2]

The management and control of these resources, whatever option is adopted, needs to take into account how petroleum and natural gas link us to world trade. We need to realize that these commodities speak within the international economy as objects of trade embody the commercial value of natural wealth. The presence of private foreign interests is also observed in their production and management.

A third economic implication is that gas and oil, along with water, are the sources of energy upon which the nation depends. With our technical knowledge, gas and oil will nourish the long-term development of the national economy. Any strategy for national economic and social development in the context of the global interdependence of nations—whether a business strategy, or a community-based strategy of self-management—requires, if the nation's relative autonomy and material viability are to be sustained, the ability to control the wealth embodied in hydrocarbons. Today, such strategic resources are controlled by business consortiums whose only goal is rapid private gain. These groups stand in the way of the possibilities we have, as a country, for productive development and autonomy in matters of economic policy.

On the basis of this economic and political analysis two things become clear. First, the country must recover the control and management of its hydrocarbon resources. This is perhaps the nation's last best chance to materially revolutionize the country's productive infrastructure and improve the working and living conditions of the Bolivian people.

Second, we should understand that no possibility exists for autarkic development of our resources in isolation from the rest of the world and the dominant economic interests. We do not need to lie down and roll over. However, for as long as the hegemony of the bosses and the transnational power of the great capitalist enterprises survive, our economic policy must conquer spaces of self-government and economic autonomy which connect to other spaces of autonomy, resistance, and economic self-management in other nations. In truth, only the mid-term and long-term quest for an interdependent globalization of workers' autonomy and economic self-management can eventually furnish the moment in which ordinary working people can enjoy the use of their wealth.

When we talk about recovering our national patrimony, the central questions remain: Who or what is the "nation"? What would it mean to recover the control and management of hydrocarbon resources "for the nation"? Who decides the meaning, and who authorizes the voice, of the "nation" that will take charge of the reappropriation of natural wealth?

Up until now, the entity that incarnated the nation, its authority, and its sovereignty has been the state. From the 1940s to the 1990s, the state has attributed to itself the power to represent the nation, its destiny, and its political sovereignty. In particular, a bureaucratic, political elite has spoken in the name of the state and claimed to embody the state. On this basis it also claimed to speak in the name of the nation. Hence, for almost fifty years the destiny of the nation has been confused with that of the state; the property of the nation has been confused with the property of the state; the welfare of the nation has been confused with the welfare of state functionaries and government administrators; and the sovereignty of society over its own resources has been confused with the state's monopoly of the economy, culture, and collective wealth.

That which claimed to possess the voice of the nation was, at bottom, nothing more than a form of state capitalism. It sacrificed the collective resources of society to enrich a caste of politicians and military officers. They, in turn, fattened up and paved the way for the current elite. This elite, in turn, spearheaded the transnational privatization of petroleum and natural gas.

That is why, after sixty years of social struggles to reconquer our natural resources, it is impossible to return to the old state bureaucracy's strategy for recovering the nation's wealth. We have seen that nationalization, in the end, prepared the conditions for the denationalization of our collective wealth. The opposite of the cataclysmic privatizations and de-nationalization of transnational capitalism is neither state capitalism nor state property. Both options concentrate control of collective wealth in the hands of a few: in the first case, the corporate bosses; in the second, the state ministers, government functionaries, and lawyers. In both cases, tiny castes and elites—in the name of the free market or the *patria* (homeland)—appropriate the collective patrimony of Bolivian society for their private use. Both, in their own ways, monopolize social wealth without the decisions and will of ordinary working people.

It becomes a question of countering both forms of privatization—the private property of the transnationals and the private property of the state—with forms of social, economic, and political organization. It is a question of organizing working people, ordinary people, and people who do not live off the labor of others and having them take into their own hands the control, use, and ownership of collective and communal wealth.

The true opposite of privatization is the social reappropriation of wealth by working-class society itself—self-organized in communal structures of management, in assemblies, in neighborhood associations, in unions, and in the rank and file.

For the true nation not to be supplanted by the market or the state, the working class, both urban and rural, and the marginalized and economically insecure of the nation—in other words, the overwhelming majority of society—must assume control over the wealth embodied in hydrocarbons. And they must do so through assembly-style forms of self-organization at the neighborhood, regional, and national levels. The sovereignty of the nation should not be alienated by the state or its administrative bureaucracy. The nation must enact a self-representation; it must self-govern through autonomous structures of participation that socialize responsibility for public life. The recovery of patrimony for the nation, the international articulation of the nation, and the form in which economic and political sovereignty is exercised is something that must be decided, implemented, and administered by all of us who do not live off the labor of others.

Now, the mere description of this concept of the nation, as the direct exercise of social sovereignty by all workers, is not enough to make it happen in reality. It requires a lengthy process of reconstituting the social fabric of solidarity, trust, and mutual support among the poor, among urban and rural workers, among the ordinary working inhabitants who maintain this country. It requires an effort to rebuild, broaden, and improve the old network of solidarities that neoliberalism has destroyed over the last twenty years. Though a difficult and possibly long road, it remains the only road by which power and control over our natural and social patrimony can be administered by plebeian and working-class Bolivia itself. The other road, state re-nationalization, is certainly quicker and easier, but clearly would mean a swapping of one set of elite expropriators for another.

The events known as the Water War in Cochabamba demonstrates that the construction of ties of self-organization, rebellion, and dignity can advance rapidly if one knows how to connect different sources of discontent and overcome the fear and the separation that isolate us and render us powerless. The Water War in Cochabamba is an example of the recuperation of natural resources by working people. Everyone mobilized; everyone assumed responsibility for recovering our patrimony; everyone deliberated in town meetings and assemblies; everyone offered their lives and their food to resist the military repression; everyone made themselves responsible—through their local, regional, and state assemblies—for controlling, directing, and administering water as a collective resource.

The same thing should happen with petroleum and natural gas. If we do not want the bosses and politicians to steal our children's future, we should help transform the suffering and weariness that has broken out all around us into a force for decision, for coming together, and for mobilization. Today there is great discontent because this gigantic wealth that lies beneath our feet passes right out from under our noses and leaves us stuck in economic misery and desperation. And the gas we buy is priced as if it were flown in from Iraq. Hence, there exists a predisposition to struggle. What we need to do is to create networks of groups that can build social unity, in which individual anger and disillusionment can be converted into collective mobilization, democratic discussion, decision-making, and collective action.

It is necessary to reinforce the consciousness and conviction that Bolivia's petroleum and natural gas belong to us—to you, to our parents and children, to the factory worker and the craftsman, to the peasant and the communal worker. The responsibility lies with all of us to take charge of the use and management of our oil and gas.

The formation of a new *Coordinadora*—the Coalition in Defense and Recuperation of Gas and Hydrocarbon Resources—could be a step toward reconstituting the fabric of working-class society. The committees or coalitions comprising the Gas *Coordinadora* would have as members any citizen, neighborhood group, housewife, or wage worker, and their goal would be to unite and to channel social discontent and collective demands. A word of caution: these groups cannot be allowed to become the top-down operations of a few who want to shine in front of the TV cameras.

The Water *Coordinadora* in Cochabamba proved able to emerge on the scene of struggle with such force because, starting five years earlier, organizational structures were built from below—from every peasant union, factory union, and outlying neighborhood.

These structures had clear objectives: to defend what belongs to the collective; to defend social rights; to defend traditional customs and practices grounded in assembly-based self-governance; and to promote effective collective mobilizations. Only this patient work—ant-like, honest, clear, and committed—could have resulted, years later, in the only workers', peasants', and popular organization that has proven itself capable of throwing out a foreign corporation, defeating the state, and, for one week, replacing the state with forms of assembly-style self-government.

. With petroleum and natural gas, one must go further and extend this kind of endeavor to the national level. But one must still start from below. Without that method, the recovery of our natural resources and national consciousness will remain impossible.

A version of this essay was originally delivered by Oscar at a seminar held in La Paz on June 30, 2000.

ENDNOTES

1. Kevin G. Hall. "Bolivians Vote to Boost Control of Gas Reserves," *Washington Post,* July 19, 2004. http://www.washingtonpost.com/wp-dyn/articles/A60424-2004Jul18.html (September 2004). These figures are based on the exchange rate of the dollar in summer 2000 and prices of $2.30 per 1000 cubic feet of gas.
2. "Las Prioridades y Perspectivas del Desarrollo en Bolivia," 2. http://www.bancomundial.org.bo/BancoMundial_Bolivia/Prioridades_perspectivas.PDF

THE LEGACY OF THE COORDINADORA

Tom Lewis

From its beginnings, the *Coordinadora de Defensa del Agua y de la Vida* argued that the social upheaval in Cochabamba during February and April 2000 transcended the immediate demand for the return of the city's water company to municipal ownership. The struggle against water privatization in fact expressed the deepest desires of ordinary working Bolivians for the ability to control their own economic and political destinies and thereby to recover a sense of dignity, both as individuals and as a people.

As anticipated by the *Coordinadora,* the militancy unleashed by Cochabamba's Water War has indeed carried forward. The various mobilizations that occurred in Bolivia from 2000 to 2003 over issues of water, coca growing, indigenous rights, privatization, electricity, taxation, pensions, and natural gas constitute the elements of a potentially unified struggle for a genuinely participatory democracy and a new economy based on solidarity and popular control. Thus far this new cycle of struggle in Bolivia's history has peaked with the Gas War that ousted neoliberal President Gonzalo Sánchez de Lozada in October 2003. An ongoing mobilization in 2004 continues Cochabamba's legacy and keeps alive the possibility of winning significant social change during the months and years to come.

FROM THE WATER WAR TO THE COCA WAR

Cochabamba's water rebellion represented the first major victory against neoliberalism. Led by the *Coordinadora,* Cochabambinos proved that ordinary people could defeat the seemingly invincible forces of global capitalism. Cochabamba rapidly became a symbol of hope and dignity for the exploited and oppressed all across Bolivia.

Inspired by Cochabamba's success, civil unrest broke out in seven of the nine Bolivian departments (or states) in September and October 2000. The aim was to win repeal of DS 21060, which had introduced neoliberalism into Bolivia. An initial teachers' union strike was seconded by a national student strike. Public health doctors voted to stop work soon after, while peasants in Carrasco set up roadblocks demanding government recognition of their illegal settlement. Striking truck drivers snarled traffic in Sucre, and a majority of prisoners throughout the country launched a hunger strike demanding amnesty. The CSUTCB blockaded the two main roads to Peru in protest over the government's failure to negotiate their demands. And the *cocaleros,* who proved to be the most militant protesters on this occasion, set up roadblocks along the Cochabamba–Santa Cruz highway. The army, however, succeeded in breaking up the protests one by one, and each sector had to stage a tactical retreat.[1]

The next major surge in struggle came in April and May 2001, when the newly formed *Coordinadora de Movilizaciones de Unidad Nacional* (COMUNAL; National Unity Mobilizing Coalition), which included the *Coordinadora* and the *cocaleros,* held a march starting from different points across the country and converging on La Paz. The marchers' demands included an end to the militarization of the Chapare region (where the *cocaleros* and their leader Evo Morales are principally based), the award of land to peasants in the *altiplano,* and the abrogation of Law 1008 (coca eradication) and DS 21060 (privatization). This action also aimed at forging and testing unity among the main organizations and leaderships of the broad social struggle.

Despite constant government harassment and violence, several columns of protesters successfully entered La Paz and held sizeable demonstrations. The government agreed to follow through on earlier promises to appoint commissions to study the effects of militarization and privatization, but nothing concrete would ever emerge. Instead, the government intensified its program of coca eradication and the use of troops in Chapare.

The following August, the CSUTCB rank and file and peasant leader Felipe Quispe launched a separate action. The peasants of the *altiplano,* who received support from the *Coordinadora,* the *cocaleros,* and the left parties, demanded a social security package for indigenous peoples, the redistribution of 3.8 million hectares of land, and, once again, the elimination of Law 1008 and DS 21060. While the government finally conceded an indigenous social security plan, it refused to budge on land redistribution and privatization.

A month later, the long shadow of 9/11 cast itself across Latin America. Neoliberal governments rushed to outdo each other in showing Washington just how eager and committed they were to pursuing political crackdowns in the name of the "war on terrorism." Bolivian water activist and labor leader Oscar Olivera was arrested on November 27, 2001, on several charges, including "sedition, conspiracy, incitement to public disturbance, and criminal association." He was released later that same day on condition that he not leave Cochabamba and that he report to authorities in person on a regular basis. Subsequently, the reporting requirement was lifted, and a verbal agreement was reached with the Bolivian government to drop most of the accusations. The sedition charge was kept as leverage, and it was only continued pressure on the government from local and international groups that eventually won Olivera's freedom.

The attack on Olivera's civil rights coincided with increasing violence against the social movements and trade unions throughout Bolivia. On November 9 in a community near Pananti, hired killers gunned down seven peasants of the *Movimiento de Trabajadores Campesinos Sin Tierra* (MST-Bolivia; Landless Rural Workers Movement); twenty others received life-threatening wounds. On November 15, three peasant coca growers died in a confrontation with the Bolivian Army in the Chapare region, where more than eighty peasants have suffered brutal beatings at the hands of the state's Expeditionary Forces.

Army troops at first used tear gas to disperse a peaceful demonstration of coca growers in Chimore on December 6. But soldiers then followed one union leader into his nearby office and shot him twice in the leg at close range. The bullets ruptured his femoral artery, and he bled to death in a matter of minutes. Another union activist, forced to lie face down on the pavement outside the building, was also shot in the leg. He lost his right leg when doctors amputated it to save his life.

TELEPHONE INTERVIEW WITH OSCAR OLIVERA

Tom Lewis: When were you detained by police?

Oscar Olivera: It was Tuesday morning, November 27, around 7:30 a.m. I was held for about ten hours in police head-quarters—charged with sedition, conspiracy, incitement to public disturbance, and other things.

TL: What do you think the Bolivian government hoped to accomplish by jailing you?

OO: Basically, there has been a very strong wave of protest by coca growers in recent weeks. The *cocaleros* decided on the Thursday before my arrest to put their protests on hold and start negotiations. I think the government's action in arresting me was designed to impede the renewal of dialogue. It aimed at provok-ing the *cocaleros* to break off negotiations. Despite everything, the *cocaleros,* who form part of the *Coordinadora,* decided to continue the dialogue. After I was released, discussions lasted until very late that night.

TL: Has the level of repression in Bolivia increased since [US President George W.] Bush's declaration of a "war on terrorism"?

OO: [Bolivian President Jorge] Quiroga's assumption of power in August basically coincided with the events of September 11. And the US embassy has been pressuring the Quiroga govern-ment very hard to be more aggressive in pursuing the coca eradica-tion campaign. I have no doubt that we are worse off now than we were 120 days ago—both economically and socially.

I believe that what the government wants is to eliminate the fundamental right to protest. It wants to criminalize everything that constitutes social action or mobilization. And they're carrying out a propaganda campaign in the news media to discredit the so-cial movements. All of this means that the government's internal war against the social and popular movements has intensified.

—December 2, 2001

The year 2002 completed a shift in focus of the protest movement from water to coca. On January 14, some five thousand factory workers, students, and small businesspeople in Cochabamba joined peasants from nearby Sacaba to press the demands of the coca growers. This march occurred without serious incidents, but police violently attacked a second march held the following day when demonstrators tried to reopen a coca leaf collection and distribution center that had been officially shut down by the government. The pitched battle that ensued launched the so-called "coca war," which would periodically flare and reach its high point a year later in January 2003.

No doubt as punishment for his role in the protests, the *cocaleros'* leader Evo Morales—the elected congressman from Chapare—was expelled from Congress and stripped of his legislative seat on January 23, 2002, by means of a grossly illegal parliamentary maneuver. The expulsion was also designed to derail Morales's increasing presence as a national leader—a presence that was confirmed later in the year by his second-place finish in the presidential election. Morales in fact came within one-and-a-half percentage points of winning the election.

The persecution of Morales backfired on the government and created a new unifying symbol for the social movements: the coca leaf. In 2002, the coca leaf came to embody the spirit of resistance on all fronts. It captured workers' and peasants' hostility toward US imperialism and the US-sponsored coca eradication program. It expressed the economic plight of the fifty thousand families who have lost their livelihoods because of eradication, and thus readily connected with the resistance to the massive wave of industrial privatizations that has led to huge displacements of workers and their families into the ranks of the unemployed and part-time labor. Finally, because it symbolized the general insecurity of livelihoods in Bolivia, the coca leaf spoke to those involved in the fight to stop the privatization of basic services, such as water, which everywhere meant rising prices for basic necessities.

The combativeness of the *cocaleros*—their willingness to stand up to US imperialism and Bolivia's national government—translated into a major political breakthrough for Morales and the *Movimiento al Socialismo* (MAS; Movement Toward Socialism) in the presidential election of June 30, 2002. During the campaign, US ambassador to Bolivia, Manuel Rocha, gave an unintended boost to Morales by publicly warning Bolivians of the consequences of voting for "leaders somehow connected with drug trafficking and terrorism." Morales received 21 percent of the vote, while the winning candidate Gonzalo Sánchez de Lozada of the neoliberal Movimiento Nacional Revolucionario (MNR) received 22.5 percent. Morales's impressive showing stunned politicians, both in Bolivia and abroad, and reflected a qualitative leap in social polarization and anti-imperialist feeling throughout the country.

FROM THE COCA WAR TO THE TAX WAR

Throughout 2002, the *Coordinadora* actively supported the struggle of the *cocaleros*. It focused its main energies, however, on implementing the process of self-management within Cochabamba's reconquered water company, SEMAPA, and on expanding the struggle against privatization to include electricity and transportation. These efforts experienced some important successes, enhancing the *Coordinadora's* self-confidence and earning it even greater moral authority. The year 2002 also saw the development of closer ties between the *Coordinadora* and the international community of NGOs. Foreign documentaries and speaking engagements throughout Africa, Asia, Australia, Europe, and North America publicized the Water War and inspired activists in the global justice movement everywhere.

Olivera himself remained primarily committed in 2002 to a program of developing the *Coordinadora* as a means of breaking down barriers among the full-time, flexibilized, part-time, outsourced, and unemployed sections of the Bolivian working class. He also sought to put into practice his vision that the *Coordinadora* could serve as a new kind of social space within which to organize Bolivian workers beyond the reach of the corrupt political parties and the passive, opportunist union bureaucracies. These efforts enjoyed substantial success in Cochabamba.

FROM "THE NEW TASKS OF THE COORDINADORA IN DEFENSE OF WATER AND LIFE"

As the one hundred thousand people who gathered at downtown Cochabamba's town meeting last April 11 made clear, what we want is not only the provision of our basic services, but also the full realization of our political and social rights. These rights are the right to be heard by the authorities, the right to participate in the administration of the common good, the right to a job with dignity, the right to use the collective resources inherited from past generations, and the right to well-being and happiness. This is *political democracy* and *economic democracy*, and for these democratic goals the men and women of Cochabamba have been ready to die.

¡COCHABAMBA!

The banner that was raised in April necessarily demands, on the one hand, a new economic direction which will enable Bolivians to reappropriate the wealth that has been given away into foreign hands, and, on the other, the replacement of the existing political system—which is based on political parties that have privatized public responsibilities and functions—by a new political system based on the social organizations that the population itself has created. The *Coordinadora* has taken up this banner, and thus, just as it will fight for water, electricity, and transportation, the *Coordinadora* will also fight to implement—sooner rather than later—an economic and political system in which human beings are neither statistics nor victims, but instead, in which they are the ones who control and benefit from the economy and political processes.

—Oscar Olivera, Gabriel Herbas, Omar Fernández, and Samuel Soria: January 10, 2002

When the coca war peaked in January 2003, the *Coordinadora* again found itself on the front line of struggle. Roadblocks and mass protests against Sánchez de Lozada's neoliberal government paralyzed Bolivia throughout the second half of January, with demonstrators demanding a halt to the government's program of eradicating coca plants. Protesters succeeded in disrupting traffic along Bolivia's main highway connecting Cochabamba and Santa Cruz. At one point, the army retaliated by completely surrounding Cochabamba before assaulting the blockades. Twelve died and hundreds were arrested in violent clashes with police between January 13 and 27.

The mobilization quickly generalized to other sectors of society. More than ten thousand retirees trekked 68 miles, for example, before entering La Paz on January 17 to press their demands on the government. Inflation has severely eroded pensions and benefits for retirees over the years, but protesters were able to force the government to adjust the value of the pensions and to peg them to the dollar instead of to a declining cost of living percentage.

One of the outcomes of the events of January 2003 was the formation of the *Estado Mayor del Pueblo* (EMP; The Joint Chiefs of Staff of the People). Though its name carried a military connotation, which frightened the Bolivian oligarchy and alarmed the armed forces, the EMP did not intend to become any sort of armed wing of the social movements. Rather, it aimed to create a space of convergence among the different social organizations in which a collective project for a new nation could be elaborated from below. This project would stand in opposition to what the *Coordinadora* and others viewed as the betrayals of the COB leadership at that time.[2]

The EMP promoted discussion of a range of key themes in addition to coca. The question of a Constituent Assembly and plans for challenging the Free Trade Area of the Americas (FTAA) surfaced as central concerns. Recuperating hydrocarbon resources and protecting the environment became prominent subjects of deliberation. So, too, did the question of justice for those killed and wounded in the social struggles. These political interests also found expression in a series of mobilizations designed to reinforce the positions of the social movements in discussions with the government.

The context of ongoing mobilization helps to explain the speed with which demonstrators came again to rock the Sánchez de Lozada government between February 11 and 14 in an outpouring of rage against the IMF. Two days earlier Sánchez de Lozada had decreed a 12.5 percent hike in the income tax for workers earning more than four times the minimum wage. He justified the tax as necessary to comply with an IMF requirement that Bolivia reduce its fiscal deficit from 8.6 to 5.5 percent. In a nation ravaged by unemployment ranging as high as 80 percent in some areas, the new tax would have gouged full-time workers by increasing salary deductions to over 30 percent.

When Bolivians learned that an IMF "structural adjustment" plan lay behind the government's decree, they targeted the national government in protest. To many, the president appeared as a lackey of international capital. The unfolding of resistance to what became known as the *tarifazo* also revealed fissures within the Bolivian armed forces and ruling class.

The conflict broke out on Tuesday, February 11, following a day of fiery criticism of the government. La Paz police walked off the job at nightfall after hearing they would get only a 2.2 percent raise—nowhere near enough to offset the new tax. They demanded repeal of the tax and a 40 percent salary increase. La Paz firemen, as well as police in the cities of Cochabamba and Santa Cruz, joined the job action later that night.

¡COCHABAMBA!

On Wednesday, a march by high school students from the *Colegio Fiscal Ayacucho* in La Paz set in motion events that brought tens of thousands of Bolivians onto the streets. As the students shouted outside the presidential palace in La Paz's Plaza Murillo, military police inside the palace used tear gas against them. The students refused to disperse and hurled rocks back at the soldiers.

Bombarded by still more gas canisters, the students withdrew to a street corner controlled by mutinous city police. As the military police advanced in pursuit, the city police sheltered the students and returned fire—first with tear gas, and then with live ammunition. Windows in the presidential palace near Sánchez de Lozada's office were sprayed with bullets as he hid inside.

The mass of demonstrators jumped into the fray on the side of the students and the city police. Protesters demanded Sánchez de Lozada's resignation and those of his vice president, Carlos Mesa Gisbert, and cabinet. They set fire to at least three government buildings in La Paz, as well as to the headquarters of the two political parties that made up Sánchez de Lozada's governing coalition. Office buildings, banks, shopping centers, and some local businesses were either ransacked or occupied in the city center. In El Alto, the poorest part of La Paz's greater metropolitan area, demonstrators torched City Hall, the Customs Office, and the Coca-Cola plant.

Two hundred arrests occurred in Cochabamba, where roadblocks again disrupted traffic between the Andean city and Santa Cruz. By late Wednesday, armored vehicles carrying soldiers with painted faces and fixed bayonets had been mobilized across the country.

During the rebellion, violent clashes in the streets of La Paz, Cochabamba, and other cities left 33 dead and 170 wounded. Seeing his repressive response failing to quell the protests, Sánchez de Lozada sought to save his own skin. He placed the hated tax on hold and vowed to maintain the buying power of workers' wages. He later sought and obtained the resignations of his entire cabinet.

THE GAS WAR

Sánchez de Lozada was finally forced to flee La Paz the following October when hundreds of thousands of Bolivians overran the capital city. The Bolivian Gas War, which began in early September and escalated until Sánchez de Lozada resigned on October 17, sought to halt the government's sale of Bolivian natural gas to a transnational oil consortium. As the protest grew and the repression of demonstrators increased, especially after soldiers massacred indigenous protesters in the town of Warisata, the demand for the president's resignation and prosecution emerged.

At the center of a month of mass protests stood popular rejection of the government's contract with Pacific LNG to export natural gas to the US by way of Chile and Mexico. Pacific LNG is a consortium comprised by British, Spanish, and Argentine corporations. The Pacific LNG contract legalizes the foreign pillage of Bolivia's most important natural resource. Under its original provisions, Bolivia would keep only 18 percent of the expected $1.5 billion annual income generated by gas exports to the US. Moreover, the contract discounts the price of gas to be sold to Pacific LNG fixing it at well below market value. The difference would mean a loss of additional billions of dollars to Bolivia over the life of the contract.[3]

It was Sánchez de Lozada himself who, two days before his first presidential term ended in August 1997, signed the Pacific LNG deal. After five years out of office, the October 2003 protests against gas privatization ended his presidency one year into his second term.

By the time the besieged president was driven from office, demonstrators had already won significant concessions. Sánchez de Lozada had agreed to hold a national referendum by the end of 2003 for Bolivians to decide whether to renationalize the country's natural gas, and he agreed to modify existing legislation to make renationalization possible. He also conceeded to establishing a Constituent Assembly as a regular component of the Bolivian political system.[4] These gains had actually been won by early Wednesday evening, October 15.

But the protests raged on. Popular anger at more than eighty brutal slayings carried out by Sánchez de Lozada's troops demanded retribution. On October 16 and 17, wave after wave of indigenous fighters cascaded down into La Paz from El Alto. Miners from the *altiplano* also advanced on the city. From the south and east came workers, peasants, and coca growers—all focused on getting rid of Sánchez de Lozada. The workers' neighborhoods of the capital then emptied onto the streets. By the afternoon of October 17, downtown La Paz was overflowing. Sánchez de Lozada abandoned the country altogether.

TELEPHONE INTERVIEW WITH OSCAR OLIVERA

Tom Lewis: What was the role of the Gas *Coordinadora* in the protests that led to the ouster of President Gonzalo Sánchez de Lozada?

Oscar Olivera: We called for the first great march to protect Bolivian gas, which took place September 19. More than one hundred fifty thousand people turned out nationwide. In Cochabamba, the Gas *Coordinadora* subsequently provided the framework for the ongoing mobilization.

In reality, though, we shouldn't speak of leadership by any of the major organizations. The people who have taken over the streets and highways have basically organized themselves.

TL: Why is it important for ordinary working Bolivians to fight for democratic control of gas?

OO: Neoliberalism has robbed us blind. In his first term as president, Sánchez de Lozada privatized everything except the air—all for the benefit of international capital and the Bolivian elite.

The wealth represented by natural gas is our last hope to pull ourselves out of poverty and strengthen our own economic base. Bolivian gas should be used first and foremost to build a better life and a secure future for the Bolivian people. This will not happen if the transnationals continue to own it.

—October 19, 2003

Along with the September 19 mobilization, October 2003 immediately catapulted the Gas *Coordinadora* to national prominence. The Gas *Coordinadora* had been formed in 2002 and was relaunched in early September 2003. This organization represented the transformation of Cochabamba's Water *Coordinadora* into a new fighting force around the issue of gas. Oscar Olivera, who in his earlier writings had clearly identified the gas question as a time bomb for both US imperialism and Bolivia's ruling class, surfaced as its main architect and spokesperson.

TOM LEWIS

THE FIGHT FOR BOLIVIA'S FUTURE

Following the October 2003 Gas War, a lull in struggle developed that would persist, despite sporadic outbursts, into May 2004. The leaders of the social movements judged that the Bolivian people were both tired and filled with illusions of the new government of former vice president Carlos Mesa. Thus the immediate post-October period became a time for making assessments and designing proposals

A renewal of the Gas War, however, galvanized masses of urban and rural Bolivians into action during May and June 2004. Marches, demonstrations, and road blockades traversed the national landscape during these months. While expressing all kinds of demands, the demand to recover natural gas from the transnationals stood at the center. The social movements, including the unions, demanded not only the "nationalization" of natural gas but also its "industrialization." This means not only that the formal ownership of Bolivia's oil and gas resources should be reclaimed by the state, but also that the state should undertake to build an industrial infrastructure that would enable gas to be refined in Bolivia. The social movements favor selling Bolivian natural gas, but only if it is sold "with value added"—that is, not as a raw material—and only if the profits flow to the nation rather than the transnational oil companies.

The renewal of the Gas War in mid 2004 shows that the fight for economic and social justice in Bolivia is far from over. More than any other issue today, the question of natural gas most clearly pits the interests of ordinary Bolivians against the interests of imperialism, Bolivia's bosses, and their state. It has crystallized the debate over neoliberalism in Bolivia. Should the Bolivian people prevail in their struggle to nationalize and to industrialize natural gas, their victory would crown the legacy of Cochabamba's water rebellion of April 2000.

ENDNOTES

1. See the report filed by GeorgeAnn Potter, "Disturbances in Bolivia September 14-21, 2000." http: www.americas.org/country/Bolivia/ DC_2000_09_21.htm. According to Potter, the *Coordinadora* participated in the country-wide protests with the following demands: "1) Final dissolution of the *Aguas del Tunari* contract. 2) Develop

and approve the new water law 2066 regulations within 2 months. 3) Dissolve the agrarian reform law INRA and replace it with one based on consultation with peasants. 4) Improve standard of living conditions, including subsidized transport fees for students, adequate public health and education and decent working conditions for people working in these sectors, review of electricity rates and tariffs, clean up of the contaminated Arque River, and full medical attention to those civilians injured in April clashes with the Government. 5) Respect for human rights, especially no construction of military bases in the Chapare and no forced coca eradication. 6) An anti-corruption campaign within the Government, especially concerning misuse of earthquake reconstruction funds and corruption in the customs agency."

2. This leadership was subsequently voted out and replaced by a more militant leadership in April 2003.

3. see P. Gregorio Iriarte, *El Gas:¿Exportar o Industrializar?* (Cochabamba: Grupo Editorial Kipus, 2003) 30-37; 54-57.

4. The gas referendum was subsequently scheduled for July 18, 2004. The process that would lead to a Constituent Assembly in fall 2005 was officially to begin in fall 2004, but preliminary maneuvering among the government and the main political parties seemed to be slowing preparations in summer 2004.

THE SIGNIFICANCE
OF THE GAS WAR

Our assessment of the Bolivian Gas War of October 2003 begins with Cochabamba's April 2000 Water War. That was the start of the evolution, throughout the country, of a citizens' movement discovering its own strength, defining its own objectives, and pursuing its own goals. We in the *Coordinadora* used to be workers' leaders and, in the old way of looking at things, focused on labor issues and salary demands. But we did not reach out to all the citizenry.[1]

The Water War transformed our way of leading—our manner of being leaders. We started to throw our energies into the defense of citizen issues. It was not only the fact that the water issue affected peasants, factory workers, and the middle classes; we realized that we could all "articulate" ourselves as citizens around this issue. That realization gave birth to the consciousness of a citizens' movement and later to the Water *Coordinadora*. During those days in the streets we learned the strategies and organizational forms that are today the repertoire of the various mobilized social sectors all across Bolivia and Latin America.

Some people who had worked with the *Coordinadora* during the Water War, and some outside the *Coordinadora*, had the idea that the departure of Bechtel meant that the water problem was resolved. They thought the *Coordinadora* should dissolve. Because of that feeling, whenever we would express our views on coca growing, taxes, or natural gas, many people started to say that the *Coordinadora* was getting involved in issues that were not really part of its mission. Although this new form of organization was born socially as a result of defending water, water itself is not the fundamental issue, and neither is coca or gas. The real issue is that the rich of the world come to Bolivia to take away what little there is that could pull Bolivians out of misery. We need to stop this abuse, whether it means defending water, gas, or the right to farm coca.

The *Coordinadora* was born out of the water struggle, but this is not its reason for existing. Rather, it exists to break the political and economic order that caused the water problem and other abuses. While some people questioned this broader vision, many recognized and embraced it. That is why the *Coordinadora* could evolve from the Water War to the Gas War without great difficulty.

The Gas War began with the legitimate popular demand that natural gas, one of the few natural resources left today in Bolivia, not be handed over to the United States, Mexico, and Chile. In 1997, in the final days of Sánchez de Lozada's first presidency, he signed a contract with Pacific LNG for Bolivia's natural gas. In the years following even greater reserves were discovered and international demand increased. Pacific LNG wanted to renew its contract to include the new resources and with a greater guaranteed supply. This the people did not want. They wanted the gas reserves to remain under Bolivian control and benefit the Bolivian people.

But the gas was given over to the transnational corporations in a completely nontransparent way, behind Bolivians' backs. The struggle to retain natural gas for Bolivians had not been understood—the people had not been heard. This shows the absolute blindness of the government, and it further exposes the greed of US politicians and transnational petroleum corporations. Under the new contracts signed by Sánchez de Lozada, Bolivian natural gas would provide $1.25 billion a year for transnational corporations and only $50 million for Bolivians.[2]

Such an arrangement—such a completely unjust investment—could not be tolerated by the Bolivian people, and they went into the streets. In the face of legitimate demands, the government brought out the police and the army and began to murder the people. During this struggle for natural gas in September and October 2003, more than eighty people—including children, youth, and seniors—were killed, and more than four hundred were wounded by bullets. This made it clear that the transnational petroleum companies are willing to kill in order to maintain their multi-million-dollar business.

After so many deaths, the slogan demanding "Nationalization of Our Gas!" was transformed into the slogan demanding "President Gonzalo Sánchez de Lozada—Out!" Finally, after a national mobilization of millions of people throughout the country, this demand was accepted by the Congress.

In 1985, as the minister of planning, Sánchez de Lozada implemented the neoliberal economic model. In October 2003 he was thrown out of the country. He practically fled to Washington.

For us this was an advance, not only because it helps to return the country's heritage—its natural resources—to the people, but also because it was a small advance toward a true democracy in which the people take control, take action, and use for themselves the riches that belong to them. Above all, it signified that people can make decisions about their present and their future. The Gas War for us means an economic and political struggle. Above all it is a fight for democracy and social justice.

INSIDE OCTOBER 2003

The imminent sale of gas to Chile, and Sánchez de Lozada's policy of handing over to transnationals all of our common wealth (what others call natural resources), obliged us to relaunch the Water *Coordinadora* as the Gas *Coordinadora* on September 5, 2003. The Gas *Coordinadora* originally had been established by us in mid 2002 and had remained largely inactive. But in September 2003, in Oruro, more than three hundred delegates from over one hundred organizations participated in a meeting. The most important result of the meeting was the call for the first mobilization to tell the government that we Bolivians were not going to permit the sale of our gas to Chile, the United States, and Mexico.

The mobilization was called for September 19 to take place in La Paz, in Cochabamba, all over the country. The overall plan was to use the demonstration to call for the government to hold a referendum on the sale of gas. The demand was for the referendum to be held on October 19, but we did not expect the government to actually call the referendum, so we planned to give the government an ultimatum by threatening to hold a popular referendum of our own on November 19. We expected this referendum would be favorable to us. This would then give Sánchez de Lozada until November 19 to halt the sale of gas to Chile.

We believed, moreover, that these three months would be necessary, given the general lack of information that existed among the populace, to engage ordinary working people in the issue. At that meeting we agreed to widely publicize the issues related to hydrocarbons and the transnationals, and to contrast the government's policy with proposals that were being generated from below.

The first mobilization was extremely impressive. In fact, in terms of a first mobilization, it was bigger in Cochabamba than the first Water War demonstration had been. There, between fifty and sixty thousand people gathered in the main plaza. It was like nothing I had seen since the Water War—a mobilization organized from below that became so multitudinous that it surprised even the organizers. All in all, more than two million people mobilized throughout the country, with major demonstrations in such main cities as La Paz, Sucre, Oruro, Potosí, and even Tarija. This response gave us a lot of energy and encouragement.

Around the same time, there developed—I do not know if I would describe it exactly as "competition"—a parallel effort to mobilize the social spaces of the struggle over gas, especially in the *altiplano,* by calling for a march on La Paz, starting from Caracollo on September 7. This important mobilization, which involved many people, sought to build an alternate movement.

The Quispe march intersected with groups of peasants on a hunger strike who were already mobilized in the *altiplano* demanding the release of a peasant leader. The peasants had erected a road blockade in Warisata on September 20. When the police attempted to dismantle the blockade, they shot and killed five protesters. That is what precipitated the dramatic escalation of events. Bolivians became thoroughly indignant over the slayings and what had at first been a planned strategy for recovering our gas resources was transformed into a gigantic mass rebellion. But the rebellion lacked unity, clear objectives, and concrete proposals.

Centered in El Alto and the *altiplano*, the protests continued to gather strength and to grow. On October 17, President Sánchez de Lozada was forced to resign his office and flee the country. There were many deaths in the *altiplano* and around La Paz, but in Cochabamba the mobilization was peaceful. Our actions were called by sectors of the church and the human rights associations precisely so that our mobilization would not result in death. We were not afraid of the authorities, but we wanted to avoid any possibility of confrontation. Even though everything remained peaceful, we did set up road blocks. People interpreted this as signaling that there existed a pole of the mobilization in Cochabamba that was ready to engage in more radical actions if the government did not stop killing our brothers and sisters in the *altiplano*.

As the days went on there also developed a middle-class strike that protested the government's murderous repression. I am convinced that, by the end, people were seeking a way out that would not produce more deaths.

AFTER OCTOBER 2003

I believe that this national mobilization was our first major test under fire after the Water War. I also believe that the lack of well-planned, clearly focused actions and the lack of political clarity and concreteness—characteristics of the Water War of 2000—made it impossible for Bolivians to recover our gas resources or bring about a profound social change from this phase of the Gas War.

The gas struggle would require millions and millions of people mobilizing against the transnational petroleum companies—the most powerful corporations in the world. The *Coordinadora* said in our speeches that if six hundred thousand people had participated in the Water War just to recover SEMAPA and to preserve our traditional customs and practices, then all eight million of us Bolivians would have to mobilize to get back control of our hydrocarbons. That, at least, was our perspective. While there were meetings and assemblies during the Gas War to discuss the issues and formulate positions, events did not allow planning with well-defined objectives, with a joint leadership, and with concrete proposals. The government repression and killing of protestors mobilized a resistance before the people had an opportunity to fully discuss and debate the issues surrounding the gas. I believe that the history of October 2003 would have been different if we had been afforded the opportunity to follow through with our initial ideas.

I would suggest that, for us, October 2003 became a process of gaining strength that, above all, made it possible for Cochabamba to be transformed into the center from where social movements can offer analysis, propose solutions, establish strong networks of collective dialogue, and raise our voices to offer a general perspective on events and future directions. This, then, was basically our role—a role carried out with dignity, with a strong voice, as a clear political reference point. I believe that this has been the basic role of the *Coordinadora* since the year 2000, and that this has always been one of our goals.

As far as October 17 itself is concerned, we frankly saw no alternative other than a constitutional succession—that is, the government's passing into the hands of Vice President Carlos Mesa. It looked like military preparations for a coup were underway. The reactionary ruling class of the eastern part of the country, which is heavily involved in the oil industry, was calling for the government to be transferred to Santa Cruz. The last thing we wanted was a fratricidal civil war.

People placed a great deal of hope in the constitutional succession, and in the new president, Carlos Mesa. Obviously, we did not share such hopes. People wanted their struggle to have meaning. They wanted all their efforts and the gigantic scale of their collective action to have significance, and so they wanted to believe that it resulted in something good. Unsurprisingly, Mesa has disappointed them. I would say that what October 2003 accomplished was to show the world that the Bolivian people are not willing to retreat from the advances they have made since 2000. This is the most important achievement of the Gas War to date. It has cost us many lives, but we have developed and maintained the capacity to articulate a concrete proposal concerning the nationalization of gas.

If we had been able to emulate the Water War in the Gas War—with a united leadership and goals—then Bolivian society would be in a better situation today. Instead, we find ourselves stuck in a fight among political parties and would-be political bosses who are not serving the nation well. Actually, it is not so much the nation as that the politicians are not doing right by the people. There are many people who have mastered the rhetoric but who do very little to articulate a real social fabric or network. This does not discourage us, but it does make it more difficult to build bridges between social movements.

¡COCHABAMBA!

We are trying to establish links with eastern Bolivia, for example, but these remain weak because there is so much fear in that part of the country. In the *altiplano*—especially in El Alto, the city that rebelled in such an important, dignified, and courageous way during October 2003, but where there is also tremendous political fragmentation—links also remain weak.

We did, of course, enjoy some unity during the Gas War. The unity we had was very horizontal. No person, no party, no labor organization, and no social movement could truthfully lay claim to this victory of the people. The only hero has been the Bolivian people. Essentially it was the Aymara indigenous peoples, miners, rural workers, and people from the poorest cities and barrios who mobilized to achieve this important victory.

In general, however, the country and its social organizations remain a bit fragmented. I believe that the leaders of the social movements, and of the political parties of the Bolivian left, if a left still exists, have to show a kind of unity that the people have shown in practice.

First, we need unity to change the economic model and to ensure the return to the people of all that has been handed over to the transnational corporations. Second, there must be a political change so that political parties do not monopolize discourse and decision-making; it should be the people who participate, who express opinions, who lead, and who decide about things that are their responsibility. And finally, we need to dismantle the political apparatus and the still intact niche that the ex-president has left behind.

The people are concerned that at this moment Bolivia faces two possible paths. One path sees Bolivia advancing in a democratic, peaceful, rational, and orderly way, with the political forces that still remain—the national parliament and the social movements—working to attain these economic and political changes. The other path leads to a possible civil war. This is the path which reactionary sectors, beginning with ex-president Sánchez de Lozada, are fomenting. Sánchez de Lozada from his luxury retirement home in the US, has declared that drug trafficking and terrorism are what kicked him out of power. This, of course, is not true. His statement is simply a call for military intervention in Bolivia. And this is very serious to us.

I believe that we still have a long way to go in developing a social movement that is united and strong enough to transform our conditions of life—to be able to implement new economic and political models from below. I consider that this is a labor that will be measured not in months but in years. But I am also completely convinced that we must undertake it. The immediate struggle will always be on the agenda of the social movements and we have elaborated our vision in the short and mid terms, but we also have to start thinking beyond the present unions and state of affairs and begin to elaborate a general politico-economic model from the point of view of civil society. Many things may come to pass before we can fully coordinate with people from below to develop a vision of what we want our future to look like. But if we do not start now, it may soon be too late.

THE INTERNATIONAL CONTEXT

Unlike the struggle of other social movements in Latin America, the Gas War in October 2003 represented the first time that there had been a political struggle in Bolivia, one in a *political* vein, which has produced the fall of a president. I think the symbolism of the Gas War in October 2003 is very important. It shows other people in Latin America that it is possible to defeat—that it is possible to get rid of—the proponents and creators of the neoliberal economic model and the representatives of the transnationals. And I believe this is encouraging, even inspiring, because it shows that the path of unity, of organization and mobilization, and of positive proposals moves us along the road toward the construction of a democracy with social justice.

This progress is organized and carried through by the people themselves. In Bolivia there is no dominant political party or social organization leading the struggle. I believe that the people themselves are self-organizing. Organization is arising from the very people who are creating their own spaces and new horizontal forms with collective characteristics. These forms and spaces are permitting people to consider themselves equals and to discover that all their problems have a common source—the neoliberal economic model, this political model of exclusion that privileges a few politicians and businessmen.

In this sense, I think that neoliberalism is creating its own gravediggers. Ordinary working people feel betrayed. As a result of the neoliberal policies of privatization and alienation, people are forced to live daily violence: the violence of being unemployed, the violence of being without rights, the violence of being without natural resources. This in itself makes people feel indignant. They open their eyes, and they begin to organize to better defend their living conditions.

The development of anti-neoliberal consciousness among the people goes hand in hand with the development of anti-imperialist consciousness. Latin America has been occupied militarily for quite some time. There are US military bases in Cuba, in Panama, in Colombia, in Ecuador, in Bolivia, in Argentina. There is a de facto US military occupation under the aegis of combating drug trafficking and terrorism that has, not coincidentally, established itself near the most important natural resources in these countries.

These developing forms of popular consciousness pose significant threats to the United States and to the European powers pursuing their interests in Latin America. All it would take, simply and clearly, is a popular uprising for the US, if it thought it could get away with it, to use its weapons against the people's movement for economic and political change.

We are occupied militarily. At this moment it is not enough to organize and mobilize ourselves economically and politically; we must prepare ourselves for a military confrontation. I believe that the social movements are quite conscious of this. The struggle will not be peaceful; it will not only be with stones, batons, and blockades. The struggle surely will also involve the Bolivian armed forces. But I believe that there is not an army powerful enough or capable enough to prevail when the people are united, when they are organized and mobilized, and when they know what they want.

I think that Latin Americans, especially the Bolivian people, have made a decision to no longer be afraid. They have decided to rediscover their voices, and they have decided to rediscover their dignity, their sovereignty, and their capacity to make decisions. Once the people have lost their fear, there is no military force that can stop the thirst for justice, for democracy, and for social well-being.

OSCAR OLIVERA

A DECISIVE MOMENT

The gas issue is the fundamental key to the economic and political future of the Mesa government and of the future, progress, and very existence of the social movements. The transnational petroleum corporations, the US embassy, the traditional political parties, the national businessmen linked to the transnationals, the local civic committees corrupted and bribed by the oil companies—all are trying to impose their version of a hydrocarbon law that favors neoliberalism and global capitalism. If these groups succeed, I believe that Bolivia has no historical horizon and its people have no future.

If the transnationals win, the country may well fragment and break apart. The eastern, oil-rich region of Bolivia has already threatened secession if the oil companies lose. If Mesa and the transnationals win, it is clear that the indigenous peoples of the *altiplano* will pull away and seek to govern themselves independently. Either path could lead to confrontation and civil war. Hope lies with the social movements of the eastern part of the country—Santa Cruz and Tarija—which, with the backing of the rest of us, could lose their fear and rise up against the handing over of our hydrocarbon resources to global capitalism and imperialism. I believe that this is our only possibility.

We are working very hard to organize the eastern social movements for mobilization. We do this not because we like to stir up trouble, but because we are trying to create a new articulation of social forces that is more favorable to the Bolivian people. The existing relation of social forces will not permit the people to impose their collective desire for the nationalization and industrialization of natural gas.

The eventual content of the hydrocarbon law, as well as the convoking of a Constituent Assembly as a space to reconstruct the country, are key to Bolivia's future. I believe that we cannot separate the two projects. We must forget about municipal elections, regional autonomies, and independent nations. We must find a way to alter the current balance of force. If we want to remain together geographically and territorially, and the majority of Bolivians do, then we need to reclaim our gas resources through our version of the hydrocarbon law. We need to fully institutionalize the public ownership of gas and other natural resources through a Constituent Assembly. In this way we will generate and democratically control the resources that will enable the Bolivian economy and government to work for ordinary Bolivian people instead of for the foreign and domestic rich.

ENDNOTES

1. Lee Sustar and Erik Fajardo Pozo contributed interview material to this chapter. Bridget Broderick helped with portions of the translation, and Marcela Olivera helped with transcriptions. Tom Lewis provided interview material and organized the structure of the essay.
2. Calle, Osvaldo. *"El Que Manda Aquí...Soy Yo:" Una Guía Para Entender la Capitalización,* 208–209. Electronic edition provided by the author.

THEY CAN'T PRIVATIZE
OUR DREAMS
AN AFTERWORD

I have traveled to the United States on several occasions in recent years, and rarely have I encountered a group of people in high spirits. The problems of the Iraq war, the World Bank, the IMF, and George W. Bush, which are worrisome to people in the US, are also issues that preoccupy the people of the South.

As I write these words I have at my side a little book which says that Cochabamba's Water War is a part of many wars—little wars that we are waging in the poor countries against the policies of the international financial organizations and the United States government. These policies aim to take over our resources and to take away our rights as people. In recent years we have had many allies from the US in our fights, but what happened in the US on September 11, 2001, has had a dampening effect on the spirit and willingness of people here to continue to struggle.

In the South we cannot separate Bush, the "war on terrorism," the World Bank, or the IMF from each other. They are one and the same thing.

I believe that we should not become demoralized, that we should not resign ourselves or abandon our struggles. They have put it into our heads that there are enemies who are attacking US citizens and that dissent is not allowed. We have to see through this manipulation of information and open our eyes and our hearts.

I think the US government, in the name of the US people, wants to make people believe that there is a victory in Afghanistan, and that there can be victories in Iraq and against the Palestinians. But these are not victories; they are great failures and mistakes. And if they were to turn into victories, they would be victories of the big economic interests, of the big political interests, of the big corporations. They would not be the victories of ordinary people.

In the South—in Bolivia, in Argentina, in Peru, Uruguay, Paraguay, and Venezuela—there have occurred exhilarating victories of people against their own governments, against the transnationals, and even against the US government. I believe that people in the US need the experience of some real political victories. We should not become discouraged. We have to raise the spirit of youth, men and women in the US.

In April 2000, in Cochabamba, we won an important victory against the transnationals and against the World Bank—a victory in which we overturned the privatization of drinking water. In Argentina, they toppled four presidents between December 2001 and January 2002. These presidents and their governments were the servants of the transnationals, and they drove the country into extreme poverty. In Arequipa, in southern Peru, people rose up when they wanted to privatize electric power for the benefit of the transnationals. In Venezuela, the people restored President Hugo Chávez to power after he had been overthrown by a plot orchestrated by transnationals and the US government. In October 2003, the Bolivian people rid themselves of a murderous neoliberal president—Gonzalo Sánchez de Lozada—who wanted to privatize our natural gas.

Victory is possible. These victories, and the opportunities for the development of social movements, will spread to North America. Given the wars on Iraq and Afghanistan, the brutality practiced against the Palestinians, the constant assault of US capitalism on the living standards of ordinary working people in the US—no day is better than today to start to rebuild the social movement in the US.

For this reason, many of us have traveled from other parts of the world to build bridges between you and us. Just as Bush destroys the bridges and highways in Iraq, in Afghanistan, and in Palestine, just as the economic policies of neoliberalism and the transnationals destroy the bridges, the links, and the trust among peoples, we have come with a message of hope to build bridges that unite people.

¡COCHABAMBA!

We have come to tell you that indifference must be transformed into militant action, into positive involvement with the struggle. Our individualism, our preoccupation with ourselves, has to be changed into solidarity among us all. We must stop seeing ourselves in competition with one another and regain confidence in our fellow activists, in our neighbors, and in our fellow workers. Our silence has to be transformed into a cry for global justice.

Bush and the transnationals cannot continue to speak in your name. At this moment George Bush, Richard Cheney, Donald Rumsfeld, Condoleezza Rice, Colin Powell, Bechtel, Enron, and all the transnationals have privatized your speech. You have to recover your voice.

In Argentina, the Argentinean people—through the *piqueteros,* the Mothers of the Plaza de Mayo, and the unemployed—have reclaimed their own voice. The Venezuelan people have recovered their voice. Cochabambinos and ordinary working Bolivians have rediscovered their voice. Uruguay wants to reclaim its own voice, and people in the US have to do the same.

We must find with each person, in each neighborhood, in each school, in each market square, in each factory and university, those things that can unite us all. When we discover them, we will have the possibility of uniting together, of speaking together, and of seeing that we are all equal. We will see that together we can win many victories.

This simple message of our experience in the South we offer to you as an example so that all the peoples of the world may have the possibility of speaking with one voice.

They can privatize our natural resources and our workplaces. But they can never privatize our ability to dream of a world with justice.

INDEX

INDEX

changes in, 107–8, 121; subaltern, 80, 82, 85n10, 85n18; working, 20, 68–70, 105–9, 111, 119–25, 166

Coalition in Defense and Recuperation of Gas and Hydrocarbon Resources. *See* Gas *Coordinadora*

COB (*Central Obrera Boliviana;* Confederation of Bolivian Workers): *Coordinadora* compared to, 83; decline of, 65, 70–71, 73, 129; leadership change in, 173n2; protests opposed by, 142–43, 168; replacement of, 74

coca growers: in Coca War, 147, 164–67; *Coordinadora* and, 36, 143, 164, 166–67; elections and, 165–66; in EMP, 147, 168; *Fabriles* and, 26; government repression of, 18–19, 26, 32n1, 146, 162–65; leadership of, 13, 32n2, 165–66; protests by, 2, 30, 31, 35, 162–67; reputation of, 36–37, 143

cocaleros. See coca growers

Coca War (2003), 147, 164–67

Cochabamba (city): mayor, 29, 40–41, 45, 51, 87–88, 98; mayor's office, 57, 59, 87–88, 90, 102n1; SEMAPA and, 91; southern sector, 87–90, 93–94, 96, 98, 101–2; statistics, 7, 16–17, 144

Cochabamba (state), 7–8, 16–17, 54, 125, 128n4

Cochabamba water company. *See* Aguas del Tunari; SEMAPA

COD (*Central Obrera Departamental— Cochabamba;* Cochabamba State Federation of Workers), 29–30, 142

CODAEC (*Comité de Defensa del Agua y la Economía Familiar;* Committee in Defense of Water and the Family Economy), 27

Cohen, Andrew, 77

Colegio Fiscal Ayacucho (La Paz), 169

COMIBOL (*Corporacion Mineara de Bolivia*), 18, 113n16

COMUNAL (*Coordinadora de Mobilizaciones Única Nacional;* Coalition for National Mobilizations), 142–44

Confederation of Bolivian Factory Workers, 128

Constituent Assembly, 64, 133–39, 170, 173n4

Coordinadora de Defensa del Agua y de la Vida (Coalition in Defense of Water and Life): assemblies and meetings of, 29, 32, 37–38, 41–42, 56–58, 125; Constituent Assembly proposed by, 64, 77, 133–34, 139; decision making methods of, 54–58, 63–64, 76–77, 81–83, 125–27; democracy and, 29, 42–44, 47, 54, 56, 77; EMP formation and, 147; formation of, 27–29, 53–54, 158–59; government attempts to discredit, 36–37, 45; international organizations and, 96, 102n2, 166; leadership role of, 45–46, 59, 64; lessons learned from, 158–59; local organizations and, 28, 58, 62–64, 125, 158–59; media and, 42, 166; organization of, 28, 56–57, 72, 76–77, 79, 81–83; participation in SEMAPA by, 45–46, 59, 60; politics and, 30, 55–57; privatization opposed by, 37, 54–55, 59, 166; professionals and, 27–28, 54; protests and mobilizations by, 30–32, 55, 57–59, 64, 72; SEMAPA reforms and, 59, 63–64, 166; social impact of, 32, 53–56, 58–62, 77, 126–27; unions and, 55, 79–80; vision of, 36–38, 59, 61–62, 78–79, 172n1, 175–76; in Water War, 37–40, 42–47, 49, 59; weaknesses of, 57, 58, 83. *See also* decision making; multitude; SEMAPA; Water War

corporations. *See* transnational

L

labor: benefits, 17–18, 26, 108–9, 111–14, 118, 121–24; composition of, 25–26, 107, 109–10, 113, 121–22, 124; contracts, 68, 105, 107, 110–13, 122–27, 128n3; exploitation of, 17, 25, 108, 112, 118–19, 124; flexibilization of, 16–18, 57, 71, 107–13, 119, 166; laws, 17, 110–11, 113–15; mobilization of, 54, 58, 70, 75, 107–9, 115, 124–28; reform of, 113–15; reorganization and fragmentation of, 18–20, 57–58, 66–69, 110, 121–23, 126; resistance by, 26, 31, 116n17, 120, 124, 168; rights and security, 107–9, 111–15, 118–19, 123–24, 126; social wage for, 65–66, 75; statistics, 15–17, 68, 105–7, 111, 113, 124; temporary contract, 122–24, 126, 128n3; unemployed, 16–17, 26, 112–13, 122, 144, 189; wages, 8, 14–15, 20, 111–13, 121–23; in Water War, 47–48; working conditions, 25, 108, 113, 118–19, 122–23, 124, 129. *See also* *Coordinadora; Fabriles;* industry; transnational corporations; unions

La Paz: in Gas War, 177–78; marches on, 2–3, 13, 116n17, 142–44, 162, 167–71; national capital, 45; police, 33, 35, 168; violence in, 147, 169, 178; in Water War, 130–31

Latin America, 15, 144, 147–50, 163, 175, 182–83

law, 19, 59–60, 90, 110–11, 113–15, 184

Law 2029, 8–12, 36–37, 53–54

Lloyd Aéreo Boliviano (airline), 142

M

MANACO (*Manufacturas Cochabamba*), 1, 31, 47

March for Life (1986), 13, 116n17

MAS (*Movimiento al Socialismo;* Movement Toward Socialism), 165

McLean, Ronald, 43

Mesa, Carlos, 148, 169, 172, 180, 184

Mexico, 170, 176–77

military: coups, 16, 180; dictatorships, 18–19; in Gas War, 176; repression and violence by, 13, 19, 116n17, 162–64, 167, 169; in Water War, 43–44, 158

mining, 13, 106, 112–13, 116n17, 181

MIR (*Movimiento Izquierda Revolucionaria;* Movement of the Revolutionary Left), 10

Misicuni water project, 8, 12, 21n1

MNR (*Movimiento Nacionalista Revolucionario;* Nationalist Revolutionary Movement), 15, 145, 166

Morales, Evo, 31–32, 32n2, 162, 165–66

Moscoso, Álvaro, 142

MST-Bolivia (*Movimiento de Trabajadores Campesinos Sin Tierra;* Landless Rural Workers Movement), 163

multinational corporations. *See* transnational corporations

multitude, 71–74, 76–78, 80–83, 85n10, 85n18. *See also* *Coordinadora;* decision making; social movements

N

National Congress: concessions granted by, 45–46; critique of, 129–31; Gas War and, 177; Morales expelled from, 165;

INDEX

popular alternatives to, 129–31; protesters and, 36, 55, 147

natural resources: economic significance of, 153–54, 171; exploitation of, 14, 131, 170, 177; export of, 16, 65, 170, 177; globalization and, 66, 118, 154; management of, 53, 157; nationalization of, 155–56, 170, 172, 184; neoliberalism and, 120; ownership of, 53–54, 59–60, 129, 153–54, 157–58, 184; privatization of, 2, 66, 118, 120, 129, 154–56; social movements and, 157, 172, 176, 177; statistics, 106, 153, 176; transnational corporations and, 145, 170, 177. *See also* Gas War; water; Water War

neoliberalism: economic impact of, 14–15, 68, 71, 111, 117, 119–20; globalization, 14–15, 117–20, 148, 155, 184; government and, 17–18, 133, 142, 146, 148, 163; labor and, 47–48, 105–7, 112, 119–23; legal aspects, 90, 184; opposition to, 125–27, 130–31, 147–48, 157, 161–62, 182–83; origins of in Bolivia, 14, 21n1, 112, 116n17; privatization and, 47, 120, 126, 171, 188; social impact, 84, 106; transnational capital in, 66, 91, 94, 156. *See also* economics; privatization; transnational corporations

New Economic Policy (NEP), 7, 12, 14–16, 120

NFR (*Nueva Fuerza Republicana;* New Republican Force), 87

NGOs (non-governmental organizations), 90, 166

O

Offe, Claus, 83

Olivera, Marcela, xiv, 102n2

Olivera Foronda, Oscar: arrest of, 40, 163–64; assassination planned, 42; in *Coordinadora,* 166, 166–67; early life and background, 1–3; Gas *Coordinadora* and, 171; in Gas War, 171; international contacts, 2, 95; leadership of, 2, 29, 31, 39; SEMAPA and, 93, 102n2; views on US, 187; in Water War, 39–45

Orías, Jose, 43–45

Oruro, 128, 178

OTBs (*Organizaciones Territoriales de Base;* Local Territorial Organizations), 62–63, 88

P

Pacific LNG (gas company), 170, 176

Pananti, 163

Parotani, 33

Paz Estenssoro, Victor, 15, 21n1, 142

peasants, 27, 53–54, 56–57, 74–75, 79, 127

Peru, 188

petroleum industry: economic aspects, 106, 144, 153, 155, 158; ownership and control of, 142, 153, 184–85; privatization of, 154–55, 170–71

Plaza Colón (Cochabamba), 43

Plaza Murillo (La Paz), 169

police: in Coca War, 165; crime and, 19–20; *dálmatas* (dalmatians), 33, 35, 37; in Gas War, 169; La Paz, 33–35, 37, 49n1; mutiny by, 168–69; Olivera and, 40, 42; Oscar Olivera and, 164; repression by, 19, 31, 39–40, 142–43, 167, 178; in Water War, 33–35, 37, 39–40, 42–44

politics: in the *Coordinadora,* 56–57; left-wing, 1, 73, 149, 163, 181; liberal, 133; party, 57–58, 70, 137–38; privatization and, 55,

INDEX

ABOUT THE AUTHORS

Oscar Olivera, executive secretary of the Federation of Factory Workers and spokesperson for the *Coordinadora*, emerged as the leader and defining voice of the protest against water privatization in Bolivia. Now an integral part of efforts to improve municipal water delivery in Cochabamba, the shoe-factory worker was honored in 2001 with several high-profile awards and accolades, including the 2001 Goldman Environmental Prize and the 2000 Letelier-Moffitt Human Rights International Award.

Tom Lewis is Latin America editor for the *International Socialist Review* and Professor of Spanish at the University of Iowa, where he is also Professor of International Studies. Lewis is the editor of *Globalization and Mass Struggle in Latin America* (forthcoming 2005), co-editor of *Culture and the State in Spain 1550-1850* (1999), and author of *La transformación de la teoría* (1997). He has also published a pamphlet on *Marxism and Nationalism* (2000), as well as numerous essays on Spanish literature, Latin American politics, and social theory. Lewis is a long-time activist in the anti-war and global justice movements.

ABOUT
SOUTH END PRESS

South End Press is a nonprofit, collectively run book publisher with more than 250 titles in print. Since our founding in 1977, we have tried to meet the needs of readers who are exploring, or are already committed to, the politics of radical social change. Our goal is to publish books that encourage critical thinking and constructive action on the key political, cultural, social, economic, and ecological issues shaping life in the United States and in the world. In this way, we hope to provide a forum for a wide variety of democratic social movements, and provide an alternative to the products of corporate publishing.

From its inception, the Press has organized itself as an egalitarian collective with decision-making arranged to share the rewards and stresses of running the business as equally as possible. Each collective member is responsible for core editorial and business tasks, and all collective members earn the same salary. The Press also has made a practice of inverting the pervasive racial and gender hierarchies in traditional publishing houses; our staff has had a female majority since the mid-1980s, and has included at least 50 percent people of color since the mid-1990s. This diversity is reflected in our author list, which includes Arundhati Roy, bell hooks, Winona LaDuke, Noam Chomsky, Cherrie Moraga, Manning Marable, Ward Churchill, and Howard Zinn.

Through the Institute for Social and Cultural Change, South End Press works with other political media projects—Alternative Radio, Speakout, and Z Magazine—to expand access to information and critical analysis.

For current information on our books, please ask for a free catalog by mailing: South End Press, 7 Brookline Street #1, Cambridge, MA 02139 or emailing southend@southendpress.org. Our website, www.southendpress.org, also has complete information on our titles, as well as information on author events, important news, and other interesting links.

RELATED TITLES

Water Wars: Privatization, Pollution, and Profit
by Vandana Shiva

In *Water Wars* Vandana Shiva uses her remarkable knowledge of science and society to analyze the historical erosion of communal water rights. Examining the international water trade, damming, mining, and aquafarming, Shiva exposes the destruction of the earth and the disenfranchisement of the world's poor as they are stripped of their rights to a precious common good.

In *Water Wars,* Shiva reveals how many of the most important conflicts of our time, most often camouflaged as ethnic wars or religious wars, such as the ongoing Israeli-Palestinian conflict, are in fact conflicts over scarce but vital natural resources.

Shiva celebrates the spiritual and traditional role water has played in communities throughout history, and warns that water privatization threatens cultures and livelihoods worldwide. She calls for a movement to preserve water access for all, and offers a blueprint for global resistance based on examples of successful campaigns like the one in Cochabamba, Bolivia, where citizens fought for and retained their water rights.

0-89608-650-X $14.00

Resource Rebels: Native Challenges to Mining and Oil Corporations
by Al Gedicks

Native peoples throughout the globe are facing extinction due to the greed of mining and oil companies. As the energy crisis intensifies, their plight sounds the alarm to all those concerned about the prospect of global warming, genocide, and preventable eco-disasters. *Resource Rebels* traces the development of multiracial transnational movements in the US, Asia, Africa, and Latin America that are countering resource extraction and providing direction for environmentalists and anticapitalists alike.

    0-89608-640-2 $18.00

The New Resource Wars: Native and Environmental Struggles Against Multinational Corporations
by Al Gedicks

    In this classic text, Gedicks paints a disturbing picture of the current environmental crisis, but points to hopeful signs of resistance and coalition that could successfully block multinational corporations' resources colonization of native lands.

    0-89608-462-0 $18.00

Allies Across the Border: Mexico's "Authenic Labor Front" and Global Solidarity
by Dale Hathaway

    While Wall Street pundits praise the global economy, workers find their jobs more pressured and precarious. Americans and Canadians are told that Mexicans are stealing their jobs, but workers in Mexico find themselves in dangerous plants where they are barely paid enough for their daily labor. This first book on Mexico's pioneer independent labor federation, the Authentic Labor Front (the FAT), shows how activists are gaining strength in coalition with their "allies across the border."

    0-89608-632-1 $19.00

Zapata's Revenge: Free Trade and the Crisis in Mexico
by Tom Barry

    Tom Barry views the crises that confront Mexico as alarming evidence of the incapacity of today's neoliberal and free trade policies to foster broad economic development. He explains that such strategies have resulted in reduced food security, environmental destruction, increased rural-urban polarization, depopulation of peasant communities, and social and political instability. This book offers personal interviews, investigative research, and analysis that

¡COCHABAMBA!

goes to the heart of the development challenge faced by Mexico and other Latin American nations.

0-89608-499-X $16.00

Global Village or Global Pillage (Second Edition): Economic Reconstruction from the Bottom Up
by Jeremy Brecher and Tim Costello

In clear, accessible language, Brecher and Costello describe how people around the world have started challenging the New World Economy. From the Zapatistas of Chiapas to students in France to the broad-based anti-NAFTA and anti-GATT coalitions in the United States, opposition to economic globalization, Brecher and Costello argue, is becoming a worldwide revolt.

0-89608-591-0 $16.00

Globalization From Below: The Power of Solidarity
by Jeremy Brecher, Tim Costello, and Brendan Smith

How can the emerging movement for global democratization realize its vision? The authors draw on history and their own experience as activists to propose strategies for building this powerful coalition.

0-89608-622-4 $13

Power Politics
by Arundhati Roy

Arundhati Roy, the internationally acclaimed author of *The God of Small Things,* explores the politics of writing and the human and environmental costs of development in *Power Politics*. Roy challenges the idea that only experts can speak out on such urgent matters as nuclear war, the privatization of India's power supply by Enron—now the center of a major national controversy over its corrupt business practices— and the construction of monumental dams in India, which will dislocate millions of people. "If [Roy] continues to upset the globalization applecart like a Tom Paine pamphleteer, she will either be greatly honored or thrown in jail," wrote Pawl Hawken in Wired Magazine.

When the US responded to the unconscionable attacks of September 11 by preparing to wage a war on Afghanistan, Roy wrote an internationally acclaimed essay, "The Algebra of Infinite Justice," calling on the world not to use violence against innocent people in Afghanistan. After the war began, she wrote another powerful challenge to the war, "War is Peace." The essays were printed around the world and were discussed on ABC's *Nightline,* in *Newsweek,* and in the New York *Times.* The expanded edition of Power Politics includes the fully annotated versions of "The Algebra of Infinite Justice" and "War is Peace."

0-89608-668-2 $12.00

Earth Democracy: Justice, Sustainability, and Peace
by Vandana Shiva

Forthright and energetic, Vandana Shiva updates readers on the movements, issues, and struggles she helped bring to international attention—the genetic engineering of food, the theft of culture, and the privatization of natural resources—and deftly analyzes the successes and new challenges the global resistance movement now faces. From struggles on the streets of Seattle and Cancún and in homes and farms across the world has grown a set of principles based on inclusion, nonviolence, reclaiming the commons, and freely sharing the earth's resources. These ideals, which Shiva calls *Earth Democracy,* will serve as unifying points in our current movements, an urgent call to peace, and the basis for a just and sustainable future.

0-89608-745-X   available summer 2005